BEYOND THE LABELS

Beyond the Labels

May we be a beacon of hope for those…

Pastor I.E. Logan

LOGANS DESIGNS
CREATIVITY KNOWS NO BOUNDS

Beyond the Labels

Table of Contents

Copyright Page

This book is a work of non-fiction, based on the author's understanding and research of autism. It is intended to reflect the multifaceted nature of autism, emphasizing both the challenges faced and the strengths gained through the journey of learning. The Word of God is central in guiding and supporting individuals as they learn to rely on Him for healing and transformation.

For information on permissions, translations, or to contact the author, please visit [iralogan.com].

May this book serve as a beacon of hope, encouragement, and faith for all who are navigating the road to recovery, reminding us that through God's strength, all things are possible. (Philippians 4:13)

Introduction

As a pastor, I have spent countless hours guiding and supporting members of my congregation through life's myriad challenges. As a grandfather, I have cherished the moments of joy and growth shared with my grandchildren, each unique in their own way. And as a coworker, I have collaborated with individuals from all walks of life, learning from their experiences and perspectives. It is from these intertwined roles that I approach the profound subject of autism explored in *Beyond the Labels.*

When my grandson, Elijha, was diagnosed with autism, our family embarked on a journey we had not anticipated. The initial shock and uncertainty gave way to a deeper understanding as we learned to see the world through his eyes. Elijha's way of experiencing life taught us invaluable lessons about patience, empathy, and the beauty of diversity. His laughter, curiosity, and unwavering honesty have enriched our lives beyond measure.

In my pastoral duties, I have walked alongside families facing similar paths. I have witnessed the challenges they confront—the misunderstandings, the isolation, the relentless advocacy required to navigate systems not designed with their children in mind. Yet, I have also seen the incredible strengths that individuals on the spectrum and their families possess: resilience, innovation, and a profound capacity for love.

As a coworker, I have had the privilege of collaborating with colleagues who are on the autism spectrum. Their attention to detail, dedication, and unique problem-solving abilities have not only contributed to our shared goals but have also fostered an inclusive environment that values each person's contributions. These experiences have reinforced my belief that when we look beyond labels, we unlock the true potential within each individual.

Beyond the Labels is a timely and necessary exploration of autism's multifaceted nature. This book delves deep into the complexities of the spectrum, shedding light on both the challenges faced and the remarkable strengths that often go unrecognized. It urges us to move past preconceived notions and to engage with individuals on the spectrum with openness and respect.

One of the most profound teachings in my faith is the inherent worth and dignity of every person. We are reminded that each individual is fearfully and wonderfully made, possessing gifts that contribute to the tapestry of our shared humanity. This book echoes that truth, emphasizing that autism is not a deficit but a different way of experiencing the world—one that can offer fresh insights and enrich our collective experience.

The stories and insights presented in *Beyond the Labels* resonate deeply with me. They remind us that while challenges exist, they do not define the entirety of a person's existence. By focusing on abilities rather than limitations, we create spaces where individuals on the spectrum can thrive and where their contributions are celebrated.

I recall a moment when Michael, at the age of eight, spent hours meticulously organizing a collection of seashells by size, color, and texture. What seemed like a simple activity was, in fact, a display of his keen observational skills and innate sense of order. His excitement in sharing his collection with us opened our eyes to the depth of his understanding and the joy he found in patterns and details.

In the workplace, I've seen similar strengths manifest in colleagues who, through their unique perspectives, have solved complex problems that had stumped the rest of us. Their ability to think outside conventional frameworks is not just valuable, it's indispensable in a world that increasingly requires innovative solutions.

As you immerse yourself in the pages of *Beyond the Labels*, I encourage you to approach each chapter with an open heart and mind. Allow the stories to challenge any preconceived notions and to inspire a deeper appreciation for the richness that neurodiversity brings to our lives.

This book is more than an exploration; it's an invitation—to listen, to learn, and to engage with empathy. It calls us to recognize that by moving beyond labels, we not only uplift those on the autism spectrum but also enrich our own understanding of what it means to be human.

Whether you are a parent, educator, friend, or simply someone seeking to understand more about autism, *Beyond the Labels* offers valuable insights and practical guidance. It is a beacon of hope and a testament to the incredible resilience and potential that reside within every individual.

In my roles as pastor, grandfather, and coworker, I have been profoundly impacted by the lives of those on the spectrum. They have taught me that our differences are not barriers but bridges that connect us in unexpected and beautiful ways.

May this book inspire you to look beyond the labels and to embrace the limitless possibilities that unfold when we see each person for who they truly are.

Blessings, **Reverend Ira E Logan**

Pastor, Grandfather, and Advocate for Inclusion

Dedication

To all the incredible individuals on the autism spectrum who illuminate our lives with their unique insights, unwavering honesty, and remarkable talents—this book is dedicated to you.

As a pastor, I have been profoundly moved by the way you challenge us to deepen our compassion and expand our understanding of God's diverse creation. Your presence in our congregation has taught us humility, patience, and the true essence of community.

As a grandfather, my heart swells with joy and pride for my grandchild whose journey on the spectrum has opened my eyes to a world of wonder and detail I might have otherwise missed. Your laughter, curiosity, and unfiltered authenticity have enriched our family's tapestry beyond measure.

As a coworker, I have witnessed firsthand the invaluable contributions you bring to our shared endeavors. Your dedication, innovative thinking, and meticulous attention to detail not only advance our work but also inspire those around you to strive for excellence.

To the families, educators, friends, and advocates who walk alongside you, embracing both the challenges and the triumphs—we honor your resilience, love, and unwavering support.

May *Beyond the Labels* serve as a beacon of hope, understanding, and celebration of the multifaceted nature of autism. Let us all commit to looking beyond labels, embracing each person's unique gifts, and building a world where every individual is valued and empowered to reach their fullest potential.

With heartfelt gratitude and admiration,

Pastor I.E. Logan

Pastor, Grandfather, and Advocate for Inclusion

Chapter 1
The Spectrum of Perception: Understanding Autism

"For you created my inmost being; you knit me together in my mother's womb. I praise you because I am fearfully and wonderfully made; your works are wonderful, I know that full well."

Psalm 139:13-14

Introduction: Autism as a Spectrum of Experience

Autism Spectrum Disorder (ASD) is a developmental condition that encompasses a wide range of behaviors, abilities, challenges, and strengths. The term "spectrum" is used because every individual with autism is unique. Some may face significant challenges in areas such as social interaction, communication, and sensory processing, while others may possess extraordinary talents in fields such as mathematics, art, or technology. To understand autism fully, we must go beyond labels and recognize the complexity of this condition, embracing both its difficulties and its gifts.

In this chapter, *The Spectrum of Perception: Understanding Autism*, we will explore the multifaceted nature of autism, examining the various challenges individuals on the spectrum face while also celebrating the strengths they possess. From sensory sensitivities to social interaction difficulties, we will discuss the aspects of autism that shape how individuals perceive and interact with the world. At the same time, we will look at the unique abilities that make autistic individuals valuable contributors to society. Throughout this chapter, we will also turn to scripture to provide guidance, comfort, and strength, understanding that faith can offer support as individuals on the spectrum, and their families, navigate the complexities of autism.

In Psalm 139:14, the psalmist declares, "I praise you because I am fearfully and wonderfully made; your works are wonderful, I know that full well." This verse reminds us that every person, including those with autism, is created by God with purpose, intention, and inherent value. Autism is not a flaw or a mistake; it is part of the diversity of human creation that reflects God's infinite creativity and wisdom.

1. Sensory Sensitivities: A Different Experience of the World

a. Sensory Overload and Underload

One of the defining characteristics of autism is the way individuals process sensory information. While neurotypical individuals may be able to filter out background noise, adjust to different lighting levels, or handle the texture of various fabrics, individuals with autism often experience sensory input in a heightened or diminished way. For some, everyday experiences like the hum of fluorescent lights, the sound of traffic, or the feeling of certain fabrics can be overwhelming. This is known as sensory overload, where the brain struggles to process an influx of stimuli, leading to discomfort, anxiety, or even physical pain.

On the other end of the spectrum, some individuals with autism may experience sensory underload, where they seek out more intense stimuli to feel grounded. This can manifest in behaviors like stimming (self-stimulatory behavior), which includes repetitive actions such as hand-flapping, rocking, or spinning. These actions help individuals with autism regulate their sensory experiences and provide a sense of calm in environments that may otherwise feel chaotic.

The Bible offers comfort in times of overwhelm. Psalm 61:2 says, "From the ends of the earth I call to you, I call as my heart grows faint; lead me to the rock that is higher than I." This scripture reminds us that God is a refuge, a place of safety and calm, even in the midst of overwhelming sensory experiences. Turning to God in moments of sensory overload can provide individuals with autism a sense of peace and stability.

b. Practical Strategies for Managing Sensory Differences

While sensory sensitivities are a challenge, there are ways to help individuals with autism manage their sensory experiences more effectively. One strategy is to create sensory-friendly environments that reduce overwhelming stimuli. This could include dimming lights, using noise-canceling headphones, or providing weighted blankets to help individuals feel more grounded. Additionally, allowing individuals to take sensory breaks throughout the day can help them regulate their sensory input and avoid becoming overwhelmed.

Families, teachers, and employers can support autistic individuals by understanding their sensory needs and making accommodations accordingly. By being mindful of sensory triggers, whether in the home, classroom, or workplace, caregivers can create environments where autistic individuals feel more comfortable and capable.

Romans 12:10 encourages us to "be devoted to one another in love. Honor one another above yourselves." This scripture speaks to the importance of empathy and understanding in our relationships. By honoring the sensory needs of individuals with autism, we demonstrate love and respect, creating environments where they can thrive.

2. Communication: Navigating a Different Language

a. Verbal and Nonverbal Communication Differences

Communication is another area where individuals with autism often experience differences. Some autistic individuals develop spoken language, while others may remain nonverbal or minimally verbal throughout their lives. For those who are verbal, understanding the nuances of social communication—such as interpreting tone, body language, or sarcasm—can be challenging. These differences in communication can lead to misunderstandings or frustration, especially in social settings.

For nonverbal or minimally verbal individuals, communication may occur through alternative means, such as Augmentative and Alternative Communication (AAC) devices, picture exchange systems, or sign language. These tools allow individuals to express their thoughts, emotions, and needs in ways that are accessible to them. It is important to remember that a lack of verbal communication does not mean a lack of intelligence or understanding. Many nonverbal individuals have rich inner lives and profound thoughts that they express through other forms of communication, such as art, writing, or behavior.

Romans 8:26 reminds us that even when words fail, God understands our hearts: "In the same way, the Spirit helps us in our weakness. We do not know what we ought to pray for, but the Spirit himself intercedes for us through wordless groans." This verse is particularly comforting for individuals with autism who may struggle with verbal communication. It assures us that God knows and understands our deepest thoughts and feelings, even when we cannot express them fully.

b. Supporting Communication and Connection

Supporting communication for individuals on the autism spectrum involves creating environments where different forms of communication are valued and understood. For example, using visual supports like social stories or visual schedules can help autistic individuals better understand expectations and navigate social situations. Providing time and space for individuals to communicate in their own way—whether through gestures, written communication, or AAC devices—helps foster a sense of connection and reduces frustration.

Patience and empathy are key when interacting with autistic individuals, as they may need extra time to process information or respond to questions. By being attentive to nonverbal cues and making an effort to understand their unique ways of communicating, we can build stronger, more meaningful relationships with autistic individuals.

Proverbs 18:21 reminds us, "The tongue has the power of life and death, and those who love it will eat its fruit." This scripture highlights the importance of communication in building relationships and fostering understanding. By embracing and supporting the diverse ways that individuals with autism communicate, we affirm the value of every voice, spoken or unspoken.

3. Social Interaction: Navigating the Complexities of Connection

a. The Challenges of Social Interaction

Social interaction can be one of the most difficult areas for individuals with autism to navigate. Many individuals on the spectrum struggle to interpret social cues, such as body language, facial expressions, or tone of voice, making it harder for them to connect with others in social settings. This can lead to feelings of isolation or exclusion, even though many autistic individuals deeply desire connection and companionship.

In addition to difficulties with social cues, sensory sensitivities can also play a role in social interaction challenges. For example, crowded or noisy environments may be overwhelming, making it difficult for autistic individuals to engage in conversations or maintain focus. However, while social interaction may be challenging, it is important to recognize that many autistic individuals bring honesty, loyalty, and authenticity to their relationships.

Ecclesiastes 4:9-10 speaks to the value of companionship: "Two are better than one, because they have a good return for their labor: If either of them falls down, one can help the other up." This scripture reminds us that relationships and community are vital for everyone, including individuals on the spectrum. Finding friends, family members, or coworkers who are patient and understanding can make a world of difference in helping autistic individuals build meaningful connections.

b. Building Authentic Relationships

Building authentic relationships with individuals on the autism spectrum requires patience, understanding, and flexibility. Autistic individuals may prefer one-on-one interactions over group settings, or they may need clear, direct communication to feel comfortable. It is important to respect these preferences and allow individuals to engage in social interactions on their terms.

Family members, friends, and coworkers can support autistic individuals by creating environments where they feel safe and included. This may involve offering quieter spaces for social gatherings, providing clear instructions for social activities, or simply being patient when misunderstandings arise. By making an effort to understand and accommodate the needs of individuals with autism, we can build stronger, more authentic relationships.

Proverbs 17:17 reminds us, "A friend loves at all times, and a brother is born for a time of adversity." This verse highlights the power of friendship, especially in moments of challenge. By building relationships based on acceptance, patience, and love, we can create spaces where autistic individuals feel valued and supported.

4. Strengths and Gifts: Celebrating the Diversity of Autism

a. Focusing on Strengths

While autism presents challenges, it is equally important to recognize and celebrate the strengths that come with it. Many autistic individuals possess exceptional abilities, such as intense focus, attention to detail, and deep knowledge in specific areas. These strengths are assets in various fields, from technology and science to art and creative writing. For example, individuals with autism may excel in tasks that require precision and pattern recognition, making them valuable contributors to industries such as engineering, research, and design.

Autistic individuals often bring a fresh perspective to problem-solving, approaching challenges from unique angles that others may not consider. Their creativity and innovative thinking can lead to breakthroughs and discoveries that benefit not only themselves but also their communities and workplaces.

1 Peter 4:10 encourages us to use our gifts to serve others: "Each of you should use whatever gift you have received to serve others, as faithful stewards of God's grace in its various forms." This verse emphasizes that every individual, including those with autism, has been given unique gifts and talents by God. By recognizing and nurturing these strengths, we can help individuals with autism reach their full potential and contribute meaningfully to the world around them.

b. Nurturing Potential

It is essential for families, educators, and employers to nurture the strengths and potential of individuals with autism. Rather than focusing solely on areas of difficulty, we should provide opportunities for autistic individuals to develop their talents and pursue their interests. Whether it's encouraging their love of art, supporting their passion for technology, or helping them explore their creativity, we can empower autistic individuals to use their strengths to achieve their goals.

Educational programs, job training, and mentorship opportunities that align with an individual's interests and abilities can make a significant difference in helping them succeed. By providing support and encouragement, we can create environments where autistic individuals feel empowered to pursue their dreams and make a meaningful impact.

Philippians 4:13 reminds us, "I can do all things through Christ who strengthens me." This verse offers a message of hope and empowerment for individuals with autism. With God's strength and guidance, they can overcome obstacles, embrace their unique gifts, and achieve their full potential.

Conclusion: Understanding Autism Through the Lens of Faith and Love

Autism is a complex and multifaceted condition that requires a deep understanding of both the challenges and the strengths that individuals on the spectrum possess. By going beyond labels, we can recognize the full humanity of autistic individuals, celebrating their gifts while providing support for the difficulties they face. Through faith, love, and empathy, we can create environments where individuals with autism are valued, understood, and empowered to thrive.

Psalm 139:14 reminds us that every person is "fearfully and wonderfully made" by God. This verse encapsulates the essence of how we should view autism—not as a limitation, but as part of the diversity and beauty of God's creation. By embracing the spectrum of perception that autism represents, we can help individuals on the spectrum live full, meaningful, and purpose-driven lives.

In understanding autism, we are called to show compassion, patience, and love. As we support individuals with autism and their families, we become part of God's work in nurturing their gifts, celebrating their strengths, and helping them reach their full potential. Together, we can go beyond the labels and see the profound value of every individual on the spectrum.

Here are some scripture references that align with the theme "The Spectrum of Perception: Understanding Autism"

1. Psalm 139:13-14 (NIV)

"For you created my inmost being; you knit me together in my mother's womb. I praise you because I am fearfully and wonderfully made; your works are wonderful, I know that full well."
This verse celebrates the uniqueness and divine craftsmanship in every individual, including those on the autism spectrum, showing that all are fearfully and wonderfully made by God.

2. 1 Corinthians 12:18-20 (NIV)

"But in fact God has placed the parts in the body, every one of them, just as he wanted them to be. If they were all one part, where would the body be? As it is, there are many parts, but one body."
This passage emphasizes the diversity within the body of Christ, symbolizing how every individual, with their unique gifts and abilities, plays a crucial role in God's design.

3. Exodus 4:11 (NIV)

"The Lord said to him, 'Who gave human beings their mouths? Who makes them deaf or mute? Who gives them sight or makes them blind? Is it not I, the Lord?'"
God's sovereignty over every individual's abilities and limitations shows that each person is intentionally created for a purpose, reflecting His diverse creation.

4. Romans 12:6 (NIV)

"We have different gifts, according to the grace given to each of us. If your gift is prophesying, then prophesy in accordance with your faith."
This verse reminds us that God gives different gifts to everyone, which includes unique ways of perceiving and interacting with the world—each person contributes to the diversity of humanity.

5. Jeremiah 1:5 (NIV)

"Before I formed you in the womb I knew you, before you were born I set you apart; I appointed you as a prophet to the nations." *This verse emphasizes that God knows each person intimately, even before birth, and that He has a purpose for everyone, including those with autism.*

These verses highlight the unique creation of every individual and emphasize God's purposeful design. They can help convey the importance of understanding and valuing those with autism, showing how faith supports acceptance, compassion, and the belief that every person has a place in God's kingdom.

Chapter 2

Seeing Beyond the Surface: The Beauty of Unseen Colors

"O we fix our eyes not on what is seen, but on what is unseen, since what is seen is temporary, but what is unseen is eternal."

2 Corinthians 4:18

Introduction: The Beauty Beyond What We Can See

Autism, much like a spectrum of unseen colors, possesses layers of complexity, beauty, and strength that are often overlooked by the world. When people think of autism, they often focus on the challenges, such as communication differences or sensory sensitivities. However, just as there are colors that exist beyond what our eyes can perceive, there is a depth to autism that transcends surface-level judgments. The strengths, talents, and gifts that individuals on the spectrum possess often go unseen, but they are no less real and valuable.

In this chapter, *Seeing Beyond the Surface: The Beauty of Unseen Colors*, we explore how autism is much more than a diagnosis or label. Autism is a way of seeing the world, thinking, and experiencing life that is both unique and remarkable. This chapter will highlight how we can move beyond superficial perceptions of autism, celebrate the unseen gifts of autistic individuals, and create environments where these strengths can flourish. We will also reflect on scripture, understanding how faith guides us to look deeper, recognize inherent value, and embrace the beauty of God's diverse creation.

As 1 Samuel 16:7 reminds us, "The Lord does not look at the things people look at. People look at the outward appearance, but the Lord looks at the heart." In the same way, we are called to look beyond outward appearances and labels. We must learn to see the unseen beauty within individuals with autism—beauty that reflects God's creativity and purpose.

1. Overcoming Surface-Level Judgments: Recognizing True Potential

a. The Problem with Labels and Stereotypes

Labels, while sometimes helpful for understanding, can also be limiting. Society often uses labels to categorize individuals with autism, focusing on what they *cannot* do rather than recognizing their unique capabilities. These labels create misconceptions and stereotypes that diminish the full spectrum of their abilities. The assumption that all autistic individuals are the same, or that they are defined by limitations in social interaction or communication, prevents us from seeing the true depth and potential within them.

Many autistic individuals possess extraordinary skills—creativity, deep focus, the ability to solve complex problems, and heightened sensory awareness. But these strengths often go unnoticed when society only sees autism through a lens of deficits. The real challenge is to break free from these surface-level judgments and begin to appreciate the unseen strengths that lie beneath.

In Matthew 7:1-2, Jesus warns us, "Do not judge, or you too will be judged. For in the same way you judge others, you will be judged." This scripture calls us to refrain from quick judgments based on appearances. Instead, we are encouraged to take the time to understand the person behind the label, to look deeper and see the unique gifts that each individual possesses.

b. The Whole Person: Autism Beyond the Diagnosis

It is essential to remember that autism is not a person's defining characteristic—it is one part of who they are. Each autistic individual is a person first, with hopes, dreams, talents, and feelings. Autism may shape how they interact with the world, but it does not limit their ability to contribute to society, form relationships, or achieve their goals.

When we look beyond the diagnosis, we begin to see the whole person. We see the artist who expresses emotions through colors and textures, the engineer who can design intricate systems, or the musician who finds harmony in sound. By focusing on the individual and not the diagnosis, we create a space for autistic people to be recognized for their contributions and talents.

Ephesians 2:10 reminds us, "For we are God's handiwork, created in Christ Jesus to do good works, which God prepared in advance for us to do." This verse tells us that every individual, including those with autism, has been created with intention and purpose. God's plans for autistic individuals are just as valuable as His plans for anyone else, and we are called to honor their contributions to the world.

2. Celebrating the Beauty of Unseen Colors: Autism as a Source of Strength

a. The Gift of Creativity

One of the most beautiful and often unseen aspects of autism is the creativity that many individuals on the spectrum possess. Because autistic individuals perceive the world differently, they are often able to think outside the box and approach problems from a unique perspective. This creativity is not only valuable in fields like art, music, and design but also in science, technology, and engineering. Many autistic individuals bring a depth of insight and originality to their work, uncovering solutions that others might overlook.

Autistic individuals can express themselves in ways that are innovative and fresh, offering new ways of understanding and interacting with the world. Whether it's the artist who uses colors and patterns to communicate complex emotions, the writer who crafts vivid worlds, or the inventor who designs new technology, the creativity that flows from autism is a gift to the world.

In Exodus 35:35, scripture speaks of the gifts of creativity: "He has filled them with skill to do all kinds of work as engravers, designers, embroiderers… and all of them skilled workers and designers." This verse acknowledges that creativity is a gift from God, and autistic individuals are often filled with this divine skill. Their creative talents are a reflection of God's own creativity, and they bring beauty and innovation to the world in ways that are both unique and profound.

b. The Strength of Focus and Attention to Detail

Another unseen strength of many individuals with autism is their ability to focus deeply on tasks that interest them. This intense focus and attention to detail allow them to become experts in their fields, whether it be technology, mathematics, music, or any other subject that captures their attention. Their capacity for deep concentration enables them to notice patterns, details, and nuances that others may miss.

In fields that require precision and thoroughness, such as research, programming, or engineering, this attention to detail is a tremendous asset. Autistic individuals who are given the opportunity to pursue their passions can excel in ways that surpass expectations, often contributing innovative ideas or uncovering important insights that others may overlook.

Proverbs 22:29 praises those who excel in their work: "Do you see someone skilled in their work? They will serve before kings; they will not serve before officials of low rank." This scripture reminds us that skill and dedication are qualities to be honored. The deep focus and attention to detail that autistic individuals possess are gifts that can lead them to great achievements and make them valuable contributors to society.

c. Integrity and Authenticity: The Power of Truth

Autistic individuals are often known for their honesty and authenticity. They tend to communicate directly and truthfully, without engaging in social games or insincerity. While this directness may sometimes be misunderstood, it is a reflection of their integrity and commitment to truth. In a world where communication can often be filled with hidden agendas or superficial interactions, the straightforwardness of autistic individuals is a breath of fresh air.

Their commitment to truth also extends to their work and relationships. Autistic individuals are often loyal, dedicated, and reliable, bringing a sense of authenticity and honesty to everything they do. This integrity makes them trustworthy friends, family members, and coworkers, and it is a quality that enriches the lives of those around them.

Colossians 3:23 encourages us to "work at it with all your heart, as working for the Lord, not for human masters." This verse speaks to the importance of integrity and dedication in everything we do. Autistic individuals often embody this spirit, bringing their full selves to their work and relationships, and their authenticity is a powerful example of living with integrity.

3. Creating a World That Sees the Beauty of Autism

a. Shifting from Deficits to Strengths

To truly see the beauty of autism, society must shift its focus from deficits to strengths. While it is important to acknowledge the challenges that autistic individuals face, such as sensory sensitivities or social interaction difficulties, it is equally important to recognize and celebrate their gifts. When we focus only on what autistic individuals struggle with, we miss out on the incredible contributions they can make.

By adopting a strengths-based approach, we create an environment where autistic individuals can thrive. This means providing opportunities for them to use their talents, pursue their interests, and contribute to their communities. It also means recognizing that autism is not something to be "fixed" but rather a different way of being in the world that is filled with beauty, creativity, and potential.

Romans 12:6 reminds us that "we have different gifts, according to the grace given to each of us." This scripture encourages us to value the diverse gifts that God has given to each person, including those with autism. Autistic individuals possess unique strengths that are just as valuable as those of neurotypical individuals, and it is our responsibility to nurture and celebrate those gifts.

b. Building Inclusive Communities

Creating a world that sees the beauty of autism requires building inclusive communities where autistic individuals feel valued and supported. Inclusion means more than just making space for autistic individuals; it means actively welcoming and embracing their differences. It means creating environments where they can participate fully and where their strengths are recognized and nurtured.

Inclusive communities are ones where everyone has the opportunity to contribute, regardless of their neurotype. In schools, workplaces, churches, and social settings, inclusion allows autistic individuals to use their gifts, build meaningful relationships, and experience a sense of belonging. By fostering inclusivity, we create a richer, more diverse world that benefits from the talents and perspectives of all its members.

1 Corinthians 12:12 reminds us that "just as a body, though one, has many parts, but all its many parts form one body, so it is with Christ." This scripture emphasizes the importance of diversity within unity. Just as the body of Christ is made up of many different parts, each with its own role and function, so too is society enriched by the diversity of its members. Autistic individuals are an essential part of this diversity, and their contributions are vital to the whole.

Conclusion: Embracing the Full Spectrum of Autism

To see the beauty of autism, we must look beyond the surface. We must move past labels and stereotypes and recognize the unseen colors—the creativity, focus, integrity, and authenticity—that make autistic individuals so remarkable. Autism is not a limitation; it is a different way of perceiving and experiencing the world, one that is filled with strengths and gifts that enrich the lives of those around us.

As we reflect on scripture and God's calling to love and accept one another, we are reminded that every individual is fearfully and wonderfully made. Autism is a part of the beautiful diversity of

God's creation, and by embracing it, we honor the gifts that autistic individuals bring to the world. Together, we can create a world where the unseen colors of autism are celebrated, where every person is valued for who they are, and where the beauty of autism shines brightly for all to see.

Here are some scripture references that align with the theme "Beyond the Surface: The Beauty of Unseen Colors" for Chapter 2:

1. 1 Samuel 16:7 (NIV)

"But the Lord said to Samuel, 'Do not consider his appearance or his height, for I have rejected him. The Lord does not look at the things people look at. People look at the outward appearance, but the Lord looks at the heart.'"
This verse highlights that God values the unseen—what is in the heart—rather than external appearances, reminding us to see beyond the surface to the true beauty within each person.

2. 2 Corinthians 4:18 (NIV)

"So we fix our eyes not on what is seen, but on what is unseen, since what is seen is temporary, but what is unseen is eternal."
This passage encourages focusing on the unseen qualities that are eternal and meaningful, paralleling the theme of finding beauty beneath the surface in individuals.

3. Isaiah 55:8-9 (NIV)

"'For my thoughts are not your thoughts, neither are your ways my ways,' declares the Lord. 'As the heavens are higher than the earth, so are my ways higher than your ways and my thoughts than your thoughts.'"

God's understanding goes beyond what we see on the surface, urging us to recognize that His perception of beauty and purpose transcends our human understanding.

4. Proverbs 31:30 (NIV)

"Charm is deceptive, and beauty is fleeting; but a woman who fears the Lord is to be praised."
True beauty lies beyond the external and is rooted in a person's relationship with God, emphasizing the value of unseen, inner qualities.

5. 1 Peter 3:3-4 (NIV)

"Your beauty should not come from outward adornment, such as elaborate hairstyles and the wearing of gold jewelry or fine clothes. Rather, it should be that of your inner self, the unfading beauty of a gentle and quiet spirit, which is of great worth in God's sight."
This passage underscores the idea that true beauty is found in one's inner self, not in outward appearances, reflecting the theme of seeing beauty in unseen qualities.

These scriptures illustrate that true beauty often lies beneath the surface, unseen by the naked eye but deeply valuable to God and those who perceive with faith. They emphasize the importance of looking beyond external appearances to the inherent worth and spiritual beauty within each person.

Chapter 3

God's Masterpiece: Recognizing Our Unique Design

"For we are God's handiwork, created in Christ Jesus to do good works, which God prepared in advance for us to do."

Ephesians 2:10

Introduction

In the journey of life, many of us find ourselves grappling with questions of identity, purpose, and design. For those who live with and love someone diagnosed with autism, these questions often take on new layers of complexity. Autism can be challenging, not just in terms of the practical and emotional hurdles it presents, but also in how it shifts the way we view what is "normal" or "typical." For families and caregivers, there is often an internal struggle to reconcile the uniqueness of their loved one with societal expectations. Amidst the daily ups and downs, it can be easy to forget the most fundamental truth: we are all God's masterpieces, each uniquely designed with purpose, intention, and love.

This chapter, *God's Masterpiece: Recognizing Our Unique Design*, explores how autism and other neurological differences are part of God's diverse creation. While autism presents real challenges, it also brings unique gifts and perspectives that can deepen our understanding of what it means to be beautifully and wonderfully made. Through the lens of faith, we can begin to see that every person, regardless of their abilities or challenges, reflects a facet of God's infinite creativity and purpose. This chapter invites families, caregivers, and individuals touched by autism to see beyond the struggles and embrace the divinely crafted masterpiece that each person represents.

1. Understanding God's Design

a. The Divine Blueprint: Created in God's Image

From the very beginning of Scripture, we are reminded that all humans are created in the image of God. Genesis 1:27 declares, "So God created mankind in his own image, in the image of God he created them; male and female he created them." This truth is the foundation of our identity. Being made in the image of God means that every person has inherent value, worth, and purpose, regardless of their abilities, challenges, or differences.

When we look at a loved one with autism through this divine lens, we are reminded that their uniqueness is not a flaw, nor are they less valuable because they navigate the world differently. Rather, their neurological diversity is a part of God's grand design. Autism, like all other aspects of our humanity, is woven into the fabric of who they are, not as a mistake but as a purposeful variation in God's creation.

Just as the Bible describes the human body with all its parts working together in unity, so too does the world need people with different abilities, perspectives, and talents to function as a complete and harmonious whole. In 1 Corinthians 12:18-20, Paul writes, "But in fact God has placed the parts in the body, every one of them, just as he wanted them to be. If they were all one part, where would the body be? As it is, there are many parts, but one body." The same is true for those on the autism spectrum—they are an essential part of the body, designed with a specific role and purpose in God's plan.

b. Embracing Neurodiversity as Part of God's Creation

Neurodiversity is the concept that neurological differences, such as autism, ADHD, dyslexia, and others, are part of the natural variation in the human brain and should be accepted and celebrated, rather than seen as something to be "fixed" or "cured." From a faith perspective, neurodiversity can be viewed as a reflection of God's infinite creativity and the variety within His creation.

God did not create a world where everyone is the same, and we see this diversity in every aspect of nature. No two snowflakes are identical, no two trees grow in exactly the same way, and no two human beings are the same, even if they share similar traits. If we can marvel at the diversity in creation, why should we not also marvel at the neurological diversity within humanity?

Autism, with its unique ways of perceiving and interacting with the world, offers a different lens through which to see God's creation. Individuals with autism may process sensory information differently, communicate in unique ways, or have highly focused interests, but these differences are not deficits in God's eyes. Instead, they are expressions of the infinite ways God's creativity can manifest in His people.

2. The Challenges of Loving and Living with Autism

a. The Emotional Struggle of Caregivers

While recognizing the beauty in diversity is important, it doesn't negate the real and tangible challenges that come with living with a loved one on the autism spectrum. For parents, caregivers, and family members, the day-to-day struggles can be overwhelming. There may be moments of frustration, exhaustion, and even grief over the life they had envisioned for their loved one, which may now look very different due to the realities of autism.

For many, the emotional burden of caring for someone with autism can feel isolating. Parents may wrestle with feelings of guilt—wondering if they are doing enough, making the right choices, or whether they could have prevented certain struggles. Siblings of individuals with autism may feel neglected or overshadowed by the attention required to support their sibling's needs. Extended family members may not fully understand the demands of caring for someone on the spectrum, leading to feelings of isolation or misunderstanding.

It's important for caregivers to recognize that these feelings are normal and that struggling does not mean they love their family member any less. In moments of frustration or despair, it is essential to return to the truth of God's grace. Caring for someone with autism is an act of love, and love is not always easy. Jesus Himself experienced exhaustion, frustration, and sadness, yet He continued to care for those around Him with compassion and grace. In the same way, caregivers can draw strength from God during their most difficult times, trusting that He sees their struggles and honors their love and perseverance.

b. The Challenge of Social Expectations

One of the most difficult aspects of living with a loved one on the autism spectrum is navigating societal expectations and norms. The world is often built around neurotypical standards of behavior, communication, and interaction. This can make it difficult for individuals with autism to fit into environments that are not designed with their needs in mind.

Parents of children with autism may face judgment or unsolicited advice from others who do not understand their child's behaviors or the unique challenges they face. In public settings, meltdowns or sensory overload can draw unwanted attention, leading to feelings of shame or embarrassment. These experiences can cause families to feel isolated or misunderstood by their communities, further compounding the emotional weight they carry.

Yet, it is in these moments that God's call to love and acceptance becomes even more important. Jesus consistently showed compassion to those who were marginalized or misunderstood, and He calls us to do the same. As a community of believers, we are called to embrace neurodiversity and advocate for inclusion and understanding. By creating environments where all individuals, regardless of their neurological makeup, are valued and accepted, we reflect God's love and grace to the world.

3. Recognizing the Unique Gifts of Autism

a. The Beauty of Focus and Passion

One of the most remarkable aspects of autism is the deep focus and passion that many individuals on the spectrum display. Many individuals with autism have highly specific interests that they pursue with dedication and enthusiasm. Whether it's a fascination with trains, mathematics, animals, or art, this intense focus can lead to remarkable achievements and a depth of knowledge that few others possess.

In a world that often celebrates multitasking and superficial knowledge, the focus and passion of individuals with autism can be a reminder of the beauty of deep engagement. In Romans 12:6-8, Paul encourages believers to use their gifts according to the grace given to them: "We have different gifts, according to the grace given to each of us. If your gift is prophesying, then prophesy in accordance with your faith; if it is serving, then serve; if it is teaching, then teach; if it is to encourage, then give encouragement."

Individuals with autism often have the gift of deep knowledge, and when that gift is nurtured, it can lead to incredible contributions in their chosen fields. Many renowned scientists, artists, and thinkers throughout history are believed to have been on the autism spectrum, using their unique perspectives and focus to make lasting impacts on the world. These gifts are not only a reflection of personal talent but also of God's creative design in each of us.

b. Seeing the World with Fresh Eyes

People with autism often perceive the world differently, noticing details and patterns that others might overlook. This heightened awareness of the world around them can be both a challenge and a gift. While sensory sensitivities can lead to discomfort in certain environments, they can also open up new ways of experiencing and appreciating the world.

In Mark 10:14, Jesus says, "Let the little children come to me, and do not hinder them, for the kingdom of God belongs to such as these." Children, with their sense of wonder and innocence, are often more open to seeing the beauty and majesty in everyday life. In many ways, individuals with autism share this childlike wonder, as they experience the world through fresh eyes, seeing beauty and significance in things that others may take for granted.

This fresh perspective is a gift that can teach us all to slow down and appreciate the intricacies of life. Whether it's the way a leaf dances in the wind or the repetitive patterns in a piece of music, the autistic experience reminds us of the depth and richness of God's creation. By embracing these differences, we can learn to see the world in new and profound ways.

4. Trusting in God's Plan for the Future

a. Surrendering Control and Finding Peace in God's Plan

One of the most difficult aspects of living with a loved one with autism is the uncertainty about the future. Parents and caregivers often worry about what will happen as their child grows older—whether they will be able to live independently, form meaningful relationships, or find employment. These concerns can create a sense of anxiety and fear, as the future feels unpredictable and out of control.

In these moments of uncertainty, it's important to remember that God holds the future in His hands. Proverbs 3:5-6 reminds us, "Trust in the Lord with all your heart and lean not on your own understanding; in all your ways submit to him, and he will make your paths straight." Trusting in God's plan doesn't mean that all challenges will disappear or that life will become easy, but it does mean that we can find peace in knowing that God is in control.

Surrendering control to God is not about giving up or being passive; it's about acknowledging that we are not alone in this journey. God walks with us every step of the way, guiding us through the challenges and providing us with the strength we need. When we place our trust in Him, we are reminded that He has a purpose for each of us, including our loved ones with autism.

b. Embracing the Unknown with Faith

Faith is often described as "the substance of things hoped for, the evidence of things not seen" (Hebrews 11:1). Living with a loved one on the autism spectrum requires a deep faith, as the future may feel uncertain and the path forward may not always be clear. However, faith invites us to embrace the unknown, trusting that God is working behind the scenes, even when we cannot see the full picture.

Parents and caregivers of individuals with autism are called to walk by faith, trusting that God's plan for their loved one is greater than they can imagine. While the challenges may be significant, the rewards of seeing a loved one thrive, grow, and use their unique gifts are immeasurable.

5. Creating a Community of Support and Acceptance

a. Building Inclusive Communities of Faith

The church has a vital role to play in supporting individuals with autism and their families. Too often, individuals with disabilities, including those with autism, are marginalized or overlooked in faith communities. Yet, the Bible is filled with examples of Jesus reaching out to those who were marginalized, offering them love, acceptance, and healing.

Creating an inclusive community of faith means going beyond simply welcoming individuals with autism—it means actively seeking to understand their needs, providing accommodations, and celebrating their gifts. This could involve offering sensory-friendly services, providing quiet spaces for those who need a break from overstimulation, or training church staff and volunteers to better understand autism.

By creating spaces where individuals with autism feel accepted and valued, churches can reflect the love of Christ and provide much-needed support for families. The church should be a place where everyone, regardless of their abilities, can come together to worship, grow, and serve.

b. Advocating for Acceptance in Society

In addition to creating inclusive communities within the church, it's important to advocate for acceptance and understanding in society at large. Families living with autism often face misconceptions, stigma, and barriers to access in areas such as education, employment, and healthcare. Advocacy involves speaking out against these barriers and working to create a world where individuals with autism are fully included and valued.

As Christians, we are called to "speak up for those who cannot speak for themselves, for the rights of all who are destitute" (Proverbs 31:8). Advocacy is an extension of God's call to love our neighbors and seek justice for those who are marginalized. Whether it's advocating for better educational resources, supporting inclusive employment opportunities, or raising awareness about autism in our communities, we can be a voice for change.

Conclusion: God's Masterpiece

In the journey of living with and loving someone on the autism spectrum, there will be moments of joy, challenge, growth, and uncertainty. But through it all, we can find comfort in the knowledge that every person is God's masterpiece, uniquely designed with purpose and intention. Autism is not a mistake or a flaw—it is one of the many ways God's creativity is expressed in His people.

As we learn to see ourselves and our loved ones through the eyes of faith, we can begin to recognize the beauty in diversity and the ways in which God uses each of us to reflect His glory. Whether through moments of deep focus, childlike wonder, or quiet resilience, individuals with autism have a unique role to play in God's story.

By embracing this truth, we can move forward with hope, trusting that God has a plan for each of us and that His design is always perfect, even when we don't fully understand it. In the end, we are all part of God's masterpiece, woven together in a tapestry of love, grace, and purpose, reflecting the unseen colors of His divine creation.

Here are some scripture references that align with the theme "God's Masterpiece: Recognizing Our Unique Design" for Chapter 1:

1. Ephesians 2:10 (NIV)

"For we are God's handiwork, created in Christ Jesus to do good works, which God prepared in advance for us to do."
This verse speaks to the idea that each of us is God's unique creation, designed for a specific purpose, reminding us of our individual worth as His masterpiece.

2. Psalm 139:13-14 (NIV)

"For you created my inmost being; you knit me together in my mother's womb. I praise you because I am fearfully and wonderfully made; your works are wonderful, I know that full well."
This scripture highlights how God personally designed each person with care and intention, celebrating our uniqueness and divine purpose.

3. Isaiah 64:8 (NIV)

"Yet you, Lord, are our Father. We are the clay, you are the potter; we are all the work of your hand."
This verse reflects the image of God as a potter shaping each of us according to His purpose, emphasizing our uniqueness as part of His creation.

4. Jeremiah 1:5 (NIV)

"Before I formed you in the womb I knew you, before you were born I set you apart; I appointed you as a prophet to the nations."
God knew and designed each of us for a specific purpose even before we were born, affirming the uniqueness of His creation in every person.

5. 1 Corinthians 12:18 (NIV)

"But in fact God has placed the parts in the body, every one of them, just as he wanted them to be."
God intentionally places each part of the body—each individual—exactly where He desires, reflecting how everyone has a distinct role in His grand design.

Chapter 4

Finding Faith in the Unseen: Trusting God's Plan

"Commit your way to the Lord; trust in him and he will do this."

Psalm 37:5

Introduction

When a loved one is diagnosed with autism, life can feel as though it has suddenly taken an unexpected turn, leading to uncertainty, frustration, and even grief. For families and caregivers, this diagnosis often forces them to wrestle with questions about the future, purpose, and how to navigate the unique challenges autism presents. These moments of doubt and fear can seem overwhelming, especially when we face situations beyond our control. However, it is in these moments of uncertainty that faith becomes our greatest anchor.

In this chapter, *Finding Faith in the Unseen: Trusting God's Plan*, we explore the transformative power of faith in the context of living with and loving someone with autism. Trusting in God's plan can be difficult when the road ahead is unclear, but it is precisely through that trust that we begin to see His hand at work in ways we may never have anticipated. Faith is not about having all the answers but about believing that even in the unknown, God is guiding us, and His plan for our lives—and the lives of our loved ones—is perfect. This chapter invites families, caregivers, and individuals touched by autism to embrace faith, lean into God's promises, and trust that He is working through every joy and challenge.

1. The Struggle to Understand: When God's Plan Feels Unclear

a. The Initial Diagnosis: Grappling with Emotions and Uncertainty

When a loved one is diagnosed with autism, it can feel as though the world has shifted under your feet. For many parents, the diagnosis may come as a shock, especially if they had different expectations for their child's future. The moment of diagnosis often brings a flood of emotions—fear, confusion, sadness, and even guilt. Parents and caregivers may find themselves asking questions like, "Why is this happening?" or "Did I do something wrong?"

This emotional rollercoaster is natural, and it's important to recognize that these feelings do not reflect a lack of faith but rather a normal human response to an unexpected reality. The Bible is filled with stories of individuals who faced moments of confusion and doubt when God's plan didn't align with their expectations. Abraham, for example, struggled to understand how God's promise of making him a father of nations would come to pass when he and Sarah were well beyond childbearing years (Genesis 17). In the same way, the path ahead for families of individuals with autism may not be immediately clear, but that doesn't mean God's plan is absent.

b. Trusting When We Can't See the Whole Picture

One of the most challenging aspects of trusting God's plan is that we rarely see the whole picture. It can be difficult to believe that

God is working for our good when we face daily struggles, uncertainty about the future, or societal misunderstandings about autism. In these moments, we must rely on faith—trusting that God is working behind the scenes, even when His plan is not immediately evident.

In Hebrews 11:1, faith is described as "the assurance of things hoped for, the conviction of things not seen." This verse reminds us that faith is not about knowing all the answers or having a clear roadmap but about trusting that God is guiding us through the unknown. When we cannot see the future clearly, faith calls us to surrender our need for control and lean on God's promises.

God's plan for our lives, and for the lives of our loved ones with autism, is often more intricate and beautiful than we can imagine. Just as a tapestry is woven with threads that may not seem to make sense when viewed up close, our lives are woven into God's larger design. It is only when we step back and view the tapestry from a distance that we can begin to see the full picture, and often, that perspective only comes with time and trust.

2. Leaning on God's Promises in the Face of Challenges

a. Finding Strength in Scripture

Throughout the Bible, God's promises provide comfort and strength to those who face challenges. One of the most profound promises is found in Jeremiah 29:11, where God declares, "For I know the plans I have for you, plans to prosper you and not to harm you, plans to give you hope and a future." This verse reminds us that God's intentions toward us are always good, even when our circumstances are difficult.

For families living with autism, clinging to these promises can offer a sense of peace and hope in the midst of uncertainty. While the daily challenges of autism—whether it's sensory sensitivities, communication difficulties, or behavioral struggles—may feel overwhelming, God's promises remind us that He is with us in every moment. His plan for each individual, regardless of their abilities or challenges, is one of purpose and love.

Isaiah 40:31 also offers words of encouragement: "But those who hope in the Lord will renew their strength. They will soar on wings like eagles; they will run and not grow weary, they will walk and not be faint." This verse serves as a reminder that even in our weakest moments, when we feel drained by the demands of caregiving or the emotional toll of navigating autism, God will renew our strength. He does not promise that the journey will be easy, but He does promise to walk alongside us, offering strength, peace, and perseverance.

b. Embracing God's Grace in the Everyday Struggles

Autism often comes with daily struggles that can wear down caregivers and families—whether it's managing meltdowns, advocating for educational resources, or navigating the social stigmas that often accompany the diagnosis. In these moments, it's easy to feel overwhelmed and question whether we are equipped to handle the demands placed upon us. However, it is in these moments of weakness that God's grace becomes most apparent.

In 2 Corinthians 12:9, Paul recounts God's response to his own struggles: "My grace is sufficient for you, for my power is made perfect in weakness." This verse reminds us that God's grace is not just available in our moments of strength but is most powerfully present when we feel incapable, inadequate, or overwhelmed. It is in our weakness that God's strength shines through, allowing us to navigate the challenges of autism with grace and resilience that come from Him alone.

For families living with autism, embracing God's grace means acknowledging that we are not expected to have all the answers or to handle every situation perfectly. God's grace meets us in the messiness of life, in the moments when we feel like we're falling short or struggling to keep up. It's okay to admit that we need help, to lean on God's strength, and to trust that His grace is sufficient to carry us through each day.

3. Seeing God's Hand in the Journey

a. The Unexpected Blessings of Autism

While autism presents real challenges, it also brings unexpected blessings. Individuals with autism often have unique perspectives, talents, and ways of experiencing the world that can enrich the lives of those around them. Whether it's a deep passion for a specific subject, an incredible attention to detail, or a unique ability to connect with nature or music, these gifts are a reminder that God's design for each person is intentional and purposeful.

As we journey alongside our loved ones with autism, it's important to take time to notice these blessings and to thank God for the ways in which they reflect His creativity and love. The Bible tells us in Psalm 139:14, "I praise you because I am fearfully and wonderfully made; your works are wonderful, I know that full well." Every individual, including those with autism, is fearfully and wonderfully made, reflecting a facet of God's infinite creativity.

Parents and caregivers often find that, over time, their loved ones with autism teach them new ways of seeing the world—ways that emphasize patience, empathy, and a deeper understanding of what it means to love unconditionally. These lessons, while sometimes learned through struggle, are gifts that shape us and bring us closer to the heart of God.

b. Trusting God's Timing

One of the most challenging aspects of the autism journey is learning to trust God's timing. Progress for individuals with autism can sometimes feel slow or unpredictable. Milestones that neurotypical children may reach effortlessly—such as speaking, socializing, or mastering certain skills—might take longer or require more support for individuals with autism. This can lead to feelings of frustration, impatience, or doubt about whether progress will ever come.

However, Scripture reminds us that God's timing is perfect, even when it doesn't align with our expectations. Ecclesiastes 3:1 teaches us, "There is a time for everything, and a season for every activity under the heavens." Just as the seasons change in their appointed time, so too does each person's journey unfold according to God's divine plan. Trusting in God's timing means surrendering our need for control and allowing Him to work in His way, in His time.

While waiting for progress or breakthroughs can be difficult, it is important to remember that God is always at work, even when we can't see it. In moments of waiting, we are invited to deepen our faith, to rest in God's promises, and to trust that He is guiding the journey every step of the way.

4. Building a Community of Faith and Support

a. The Power of Community in Navigating Autism

Living with autism can sometimes feel isolating, both for individuals on the spectrum and for their families. The unique challenges of autism can make it difficult to fit into social or community settings that are designed with neurotypical individuals in mind. However, it is in these moments of isolation that the power of community becomes even more important.

The Bible emphasizes the importance of community in the life of faith. In Galatians 6:2, we are called to "carry each other's burdens, and in this way you will fulfill the law of Christ." For families living with autism, this means that we are not meant to walk this journey alone. Building a community of faith and support—whether through church, support groups, or friendships—provides the encouragement, strength, and practical help needed to navigate the complexities of autism.

Faith communities, in particular, can play a vital role in supporting families affected by autism. Churches can offer respite care, provide sensory-friendly services, and create inclusive environments where individuals with autism are welcomed and valued. By fostering a spirit of compassion, understanding, and inclusion, the church can be a place where families feel supported in their faith and their daily struggles.

b. The Role of Prayer and Spiritual Support

Prayer is a powerful tool for navigating the uncertainties and challenges of autism. Through prayer, we invite God into our struggles, our fears, and our hopes, trusting that He hears us and is working on our behalf. Philippians 4:6-7 reminds us, "Do not be anxious about anything, but in every situation, by prayer and petition, with thanksgiving, present your requests to God. And the peace of God, which transcends all understanding, will guard your hearts and your minds in Christ Jesus."

For families living with autism, prayer offers a space to release anxiety, to seek God's guidance, and to find peace in the midst of challenges. Whether it's praying for patience, wisdom, or strength, bringing our needs before God allows us to experience His comfort and presence in tangible ways.

In addition to personal prayer, seeking spiritual support from others can be a source of encouragement and strength. Whether through prayer circles, church groups, or close friends, inviting others to pray alongside you creates a sense of community and reminds you that you are not alone in your journey. God works through the prayers of His people, and by leaning on the support of others, families can experience the power of collective faith.

5. Surrendering Control: Letting Go and Letting God

a. The Importance of Surrender in the Faith Journey

Surrendering control is one of the most difficult aspects of the faith journey, especially when it comes to the well-being of a loved one with autism. As parents, caregivers, or family members, the instinct to protect, guide, and ensure the best outcomes for our loved ones is strong. However, there comes a point when we must acknowledge that we cannot control every aspect of their journey or their future.

In Matthew 6:34, Jesus reminds us, "Therefore do not worry about tomorrow, for tomorrow will worry about itself. Each day has enough trouble of its own." Surrendering control means releasing the need to manage every detail of the future and instead trusting that God holds our loved ones in His hands. This doesn't mean we stop advocating for their needs or seeking the best resources, but it does mean that we trust God's plan is greater than our own.

Letting go and letting God is not about giving up—it's about recognizing that God's love for our loved ones is even greater than our own. He knows their needs, their future, and their hearts better than we ever could, and He is faithfully guiding their path.

b. Finding Peace in God's Sovereignty

God's sovereignty means that He is in control of all things, and nothing happens outside of His will. While this concept can be difficult to grasp, especially in the face of challenges, it offers a deep sense of peace when we fully embrace it. Romans 8:28 reminds us, "And we know that in all things God works for the good of those who love him, who have been called according to his purpose."

Even when we don't understand why certain challenges arise or why progress seems slow, we can trust that God is working all things together for good. His plan is not always immediately clear, but His sovereignty assures us that nothing is wasted, and every moment—both the joyful and the difficult—is part of His divine purpose.

Finding peace in God's sovereignty allows us to rest in the knowledge that we don't have to have all the answers. We can trust that God is in control and that His plan for our loved ones is unfolding in His perfect timing.

Conclusion: Finding Faith in the Unseen

Living with and loving someone with autism is a journey of both challenges and blessings. It is a journey that requires deep faith, patience, and trust in God's plan. While the road may be uncertain, and the future may not always be clear, faith invites us to trust that God is with us every step of the way. His plan for our lives, and for the lives of our loved ones with autism, is one of purpose, love, and grace.

As we navigate the complexities of autism, we are called to surrender our need for control, to lean on God's promises, and to find peace in His sovereignty. Through prayer, community, and a deepening trust in God's goodness, we can find the strength to continue moving forward, knowing that God's plan is greater than we can imagine. Faith in the unseen is not about having all the answers—it's about trusting that God's hand is at work, weaving a tapestry of grace, purpose, and love that will one day be revealed in full. In the end, we are reminded that, despite the struggles and uncertainties, God is faithful, and His plan for each of us is perfect.

Here are some scripture references that align with the theme "Finding Faith in the Unseen: Trusting God's Plan" for Chapter 1:

1. Hebrews 11:1 (NIV)

"Now faith is confidence in what we hope for and assurance about what we do not see."
This foundational verse emphasizes that faith involves trusting in what we cannot see, reinforcing the concept of believing in God's unseen plan.

2. 2 Corinthians 5:7 (NIV)

"For we live by faith, not by sight."
This verse reminds us that our journey with God requires walking by faith, even when we cannot see the full picture, trusting His guidance along the way.

3. Jeremiah 29:11 (NIV)

"'For I know the plans I have for you,' declares the Lord, 'plans to prosper you and not to harm you, plans to give you hope and a future.'"
God reassures us that He has a plan for our lives, even if we cannot always see or understand it in the moment, encouraging us to trust in His future for us.

4. Proverbs 3:5-6 (NIV)

"Trust in the Lord with all your heart and lean not on your own understanding; in all your ways submit to him, and he will make your paths straight."
This passage encourages us to trust in God rather than our own understanding, reinforcing the idea that faith is about surrendering control and believing in God's greater plan.

5. Isaiah 55:8-9 (NIV)

"'For my thoughts are not your thoughts, neither are your ways my ways,' declares the Lord. 'As the heavens are higher than the earth, so are my ways higher than your ways and my thoughts than your thoughts.'"
God's plans and thoughts are beyond our comprehension, reminding us to have faith in His higher ways, even when they seem mysterious or unseen.

These scriptures emphasize the importance of trusting in God's unseen plan, reminding us that faith involves relying on His wisdom, timing, and promises even when we cannot see the full picture.

Chapter 5

The Language of Silence: Communicating with God

"He says, 'Be still, and know that I am God; I will be exalted among the nations, I will be exalted in the earth."

Psalm 46:10

Introduction

Communication is often considered the bedrock of human connection. It's through words, gestures, and expressions that we convey our thoughts, emotions, and needs to one another. For families and caregivers of loved ones diagnosed with autism, communication can present both unique challenges and profound opportunities for growth. Autism often affects the ability to communicate in traditional ways—some individuals may be nonverbal, while others might struggle with the subtleties of social interactions. Yet, amidst the challenge of finding a common language with a loved one on the autism spectrum, another form of communication begins to take shape: the language of silence.

The language of silence is not just about the absence of words. It's about the deep, often unspoken connection we can cultivate with one another and with God. Silence has a power all its own—it's in the pauses, in the quiet moments, and in the spaces where words fail but understanding still exists. This chapter, *The Language of Silence: Communicating with God*, delves into how silence plays a significant role in communicating with both our loved ones with autism and with God. It explores how moments of quiet reflection, prayer, and presence can deepen our relationships and offer a pathway to communion with the divine, even when verbal communication feels limited or strained.

1. Silence as a Form of Communication in Autism

a. The Quiet Struggles of Nonverbal Communication

One of the most profound challenges that families and caregivers of individuals with autism often face is the difficulty in communication. For some, autism can affect the ability to speak at all, leading to nonverbal forms of communication that require patience, understanding, and creativity. A loved one who does not use words may communicate in ways that are subtler—through body language, eye contact (or lack thereof), gestures, or behaviors. While these forms of communication may seem quiet on the surface, they are rich with meaning when approached with the right heart and mindset.

Nonverbal communication in autism is not a void or absence; it is an invitation to slow down and listen with more than just our ears. It calls us to attune ourselves to the nuances of expression that might otherwise go unnoticed—the slight touch of a hand, the turn of a head, or the soft hum of a favorite tune. Each gesture carries its own significance, its own language.

Just as we learn to understand our loved ones in these quieter moments, we can also learn to understand God's voice in the silence. There is a deep connection between learning to communicate with a loved one with autism and learning to communicate with God. Both require us to quiet our minds, open our hearts, and listen beyond the surface.

b. Learning to Speak Without Words

In many ways, autism teaches us that communication is not confined to words. Nonverbal individuals often find ways to connect that are equally powerful and intimate. Whether through the use of assistive devices, gestures, or simply the presence of shared time, communication takes on a new meaning. It's about presence, about being there and offering the gift of attention and love in a way that words might not always express.

As we learn to communicate with our loved ones in these ways, we begin to see parallels in how God communicates with us. There are moments in life when we may not have the words to express our emotions, our prayers, or our needs. In those moments, silence becomes our language. Romans 8:26 offers comfort in these moments, saying, "The Spirit helps us in our weakness. We do not know what we ought to pray for, but the Spirit himself intercedes for us through wordless groans." Just as we learn to communicate without words with our loved ones, we find that God understands us fully, even in our silence.

2. Silence as Sacred Space: Finding God in Stillness

a. The Biblical Call to Silence

Throughout the Bible, silence is often portrayed as a sacred space—a moment where the divine and human meet in quiet reflection. Silence is not the absence of sound, but the presence of peace and stillness. In Psalm 46:10, we are reminded to "Be still, and know that I am God." This verse points to the power of quieting our minds and hearts to become aware of God's presence in ways that we might miss in the noise and busyness of life.

In the context of caring for a loved one with autism, finding moments of stillness can feel elusive. The demands of caregiving, navigating sensory sensitivities, and managing routines often leave little room for quiet. Yet, it is in these very moments of quiet—perhaps during a pause in the day, a walk with a loved one, or even the gentle rhythms of routine—that we can find a deep connection with God.

God speaks to us in the stillness. In 1 Kings 19:12, Elijah encounters God not in the mighty wind, earthquake, or fire, but in a gentle whisper. Just as we attune ourselves to the subtleties of our loved ones' nonverbal communication, we are invited to tune in to the quiet ways God speaks into our lives. His presence is often found not in the grand gestures but in the small, quiet moments that remind us of His love and guidance.

b. The Power of Silent Prayer

Prayer is often thought of as a conversation with God, where we express our thoughts, requests, and gratitude. However, silent prayer—prayer without words—is an equally powerful way of communicating with God. Silent prayer invites us to simply be in God's presence, to listen rather than speak, and to trust that God hears the deepest desires of our hearts, even when we cannot articulate them.

For families living with autism, silent prayer can be a source of profound comfort. In moments of exhaustion or uncertainty, when words fail us, we can sit in silence before God, trusting that He knows our needs before we even ask. Matthew 6:8 reassures us that "your Father knows what you need before you ask him." This assurance allows us to release the pressure to always find the right words and instead rest in the quiet confidence that God hears the prayers we cannot speak.

In these moments of silent prayer, we also begin to see parallels with the silent ways our loved ones communicate. Just as we learn to understand the unspoken language of our loved ones, we come to trust that God understands us even when we don't have the words. Silence becomes a bridge that connects us to both our loved ones and to God in deeper, more intimate ways.

3. Presence Over Words: The Ministry of Being Present

a. The Gift of Presence in Autism

One of the most powerful lessons we can learn from living with a loved one with autism is the value of presence. In a world that often prioritizes verbal communication and active engagement, we are reminded that simply being present with someone—whether or not words are exchanged—can be a profound act of love.

For many individuals with autism, verbal communication may not be their preferred or strongest way of connecting. Instead, they may communicate through their actions, their interests, or simply through their presence. For families and caregivers, learning to value and honor this type of communication means understanding that presence can speak louder than words.

Sitting quietly with a loved one, engaging in their favorite activities, or simply being near them without the expectation of conversation can be deeply meaningful. It is in these moments that we see the beauty of silent connection—of love expressed without words, of communion shared through presence.

In the same way, God calls us to be present with Him. He doesn't always require us to come to Him with words or actions. Sometimes, He simply invites us to sit with Him, to be still, and to rest in His presence. Psalm 131:2 illustrates this beautifully: "But I have calmed and quieted myself, I am like a weaned child with its mother; like a weaned child I am content." This imagery of a child resting in the quiet presence of a parent reflects the peace we can find when we are present with God, even without words.

b. The Ministry of Presence

Just as presence is a gift we give to our loved ones with autism, it is also a ministry we offer to others in times of need. When we accompany someone through a difficult time, we may not always have the right words to say, but our presence alone can provide comfort and reassurance. This is often called the "ministry of presence"—the idea that simply being there, listening, or sitting in silence with someone can be an act of profound love and support.

In John 11:35, the shortest verse in the Bible, we see the power of presence in action. "Jesus wept." These two words, though brief, show us that Jesus did not rush to offer explanations or solutions when faced with the grief of His friends. Instead, He was present with them in their sorrow. He sat with them in their pain, shared their grief, and wept alongside them. This act of presence was a powerful demonstration of His love and empathy.

For families of individuals with autism, the ministry of presence takes on a special meaning. It reminds us that we don't always need to "fix" things or find solutions for every challenge. Sometimes, the most loving thing we can do is to simply be there—to sit in the silence, to walk alongside our loved ones, and to trust that God's presence is with us, even in the quiet.

4. Listening for God's Voice in the Silence

a. The Discipline of Listening

Listening is an essential part of communication, yet it's often the most challenging. In a world filled with noise, distractions, and constant stimulation, learning to listen—truly listen—is a discipline that requires intentionality. For families of individuals with autism, listening goes beyond hearing words. It involves paying attention to subtle cues, understanding nonverbal expressions, and being attuned to the emotional and sensory needs of our loved ones.

In our relationship with God, listening is just as important. We often approach prayer as a one-sided conversation, where we present our requests, needs, and concerns to God. But prayer is also about listening—listening for God's guidance, His comfort, and His direction in our lives. This requires us to cultivate stillness, to quiet our hearts and minds, and to create space for God to speak.

In 1 Samuel 3:10, young Samuel learns the importance of listening to God when he responds, "Speak, Lord, for your servant is listening." This posture of openness and receptivity is one that we are called to adopt in our own spiritual lives. Just as we learn to listen to our loved ones with autism, we must also learn to listen to God in the silence. His voice may not come in thunderous proclamations but in the gentle whispers that require us to be still and attentive.

b. The Still Small Voice of God

God's voice is often described as a "still small voice" or a gentle whisper, as seen in the story of Elijah in 1 Kings 19:11-12. After the wind, the earthquake, and the fire, it was in the quiet that Elijah heard God speak. This reminds us that God's voice is not always loud or obvious; it often comes in the moments of stillness, in the spaces where we least expect it.

For those caring for a loved one with autism, these moments of quiet can feel few and far between. The demands of caregiving, managing sensory sensitivities, and navigating daily routines can leave little room for stillness. Yet, it is precisely in these moments of chaos and noise that God's still small voice can break through, offering peace, guidance, and reassurance.

By creating intentional moments of quiet—whether through silent prayer, meditation, or simply taking a few moments to breathe—we open ourselves to hearing God's voice. These moments don't have to be long or elaborate; even a brief pause in the day can become an opportunity for connection with the divine. In these pauses, we are reminded that God is with us, guiding us through every challenge and every moment of silence.

5. Silence as a Path to Healing and Transformation

a. The Healing Power of Silence

Silence has a unique capacity to bring healing—both to our relationships and to our souls. In silence, we find space to reflect, to process, and to let go of the noise and distractions that often cloud our thoughts. For individuals with autism, silence can be a refuge from the sensory overload of the world—a space where they can find peace and clarity.

For caregivers and family members, silence can also be a source of healing. In the quiet moments, we can release the pressures and expectations we place on ourselves. We can let go of the need to always have the right words or the perfect solutions. Instead, we can rest in the knowledge that God is present with us, offering His love and grace in the silence.

In Matthew 11:28, Jesus invites us to find rest in Him, saying, "Come to me, all you who are weary and burdened, and I will give you rest." This invitation is a reminder that we don't have to carry the weight of our challenges alone. In the silence, we can bring our burdens to God and find rest in His presence.

b. Transformation Through Silence

Silence is not only a space for healing; it is also a space for transformation. In the quiet, we are able to hear God's voice more clearly, to reflect on His word, and to allow His presence to shape and transform us. Just as a seed grows in the quiet of the soil, our faith and our relationships with God and our loved ones grow in the moments of stillness.

For families living with autism, this transformation may come in unexpected ways. It may be the transformation of how we see our loved ones—not as individuals to be fixed or changed, but as beautiful reflections of God's creativity and love. It may be the transformation of our understanding of communication, learning that words are not always necessary for deep connection. Or it may be the transformation of our own hearts, as we learn to trust God more fully in the silence.

In 2 Corinthians 3:18, we are reminded that "we all, who with unveiled faces contemplate the Lord's glory, are being transformed into his image with ever-increasing glory." This transformation happens as we draw near to God, as we listen for His voice, and as we allow His presence to shape us in the quiet moments.

Conclusion: The Sacred Language of Silence

In the journey of living with and loving someone with autism, we learn that silence is not an absence but a presence—a sacred space where connection, understanding, and love can flourish. The language of silence invites us to slow down, to listen with our hearts, and to trust that communication does not always require words. Just as we learn to communicate with our loved ones in ways that go beyond speech, we learn to communicate with God in the stillness, knowing that He hears us even when we cannot find the words to speak.

As we embrace the language of silence, we discover that it is a pathway to deeper relationships—with our loved ones, with ourselves, and with God. It is in the quiet moments, in the pauses between words, that we find the presence of God most profoundly. Through silence, we are invited to trust in God's plan, to rest in His love, and to experience the beauty of connection that transcends words.

Here are some scripture references that align with the theme "The Language of Silence: Communicating with God" for Chapter 1:

1. Psalm 46:10 (NIV)

"He says, 'Be still, and know that I am God; I will be exalted among the nations, I will be exalted in the earth.'"
This verse highlights the importance of stillness and silence, reminding us that in the quiet, we can recognize and communicate with God.

2. 1 Kings 19:11-12 (NIV)

"The Lord said, 'Go out and stand on the mountain in the presence of the Lord, for the Lord is about to pass by.' Then a great and powerful wind tore the mountains apart and shattered the rocks before the Lord, but the Lord was not in the wind. After the wind

there was an earthquake, but the Lord was not in the earthquake. After the earthquake came a fire, but the Lord was not in the fire. And after the fire came a gentle whisper."
This passage shows that God often speaks in a gentle whisper, or in silence, rather than through loud or dramatic means, teaching us to listen for Him in quiet moments.

3. Habakkuk 2:20 (NIV)

"The Lord is in his holy temple; let all the earth be silent before him."
This verse emphasizes the reverence and silence we are called to observe in God's presence, showing that silence can be a form of deep communication with Him.

4. Psalm 62:5 (NIV)

"Yes, my soul, find rest in God; my hope comes from him."
In silence and stillness, we find rest and hope in God. This verse reflects the idea that silence allows us to connect more deeply with God's presence and guidance.

5. Lamentations 3:26 (NIV)

"It is good to wait quietly for the salvation of the Lord."
Waiting quietly and patiently is a key part of communicating with God, trusting in His timing and salvation through silent faith.

These scriptures emphasize the power of silence in communicating with God, encouraging us to find Him in stillness and to trust His voice in moments of quiet reflection.

Chapter 6

Friendships and Relationships: Building Meaningful Connections

"Above all, love each other deeply, because love covers over a multitude of sins. Offer hospitality to one another without grumbling. Each of you should use whatever gift you have received to serve others, as faithful stewards of God's grace in its various forms."

1 Peter 4:8-10

Introduction: The Heart of Connection

Human beings are created with an intrinsic need for connection. Friendships and relationships not only provide companionship, but they also give us a sense of purpose, belonging, and love. For individuals on the autism spectrum, building these connections can be challenging, but it is no less essential. Autism may impact how individuals perceive social cues, understand communication, or engage with others, but it does not diminish their desire to form meaningful relationships or their capacity to offer love, loyalty, and support.

In this chapter, *Friendships and Relationships: Building Meaningful Connections*, we will explore the unique ways that individuals with autism experience and navigate friendships and relationships. From communication challenges to sensory sensitivities, we will examine both the obstacles and the strengths that people on the spectrum bring to their social interactions. Moreover, we will turn to scripture to offer guidance on how to foster meaningful connections grounded in patience, empathy, and love, following the example set by God's word.

The Bible offers timeless wisdom on relationships. Proverbs 18:24 reminds us that "one who has unreliable friends soon comes to ruin, but there is a friend who sticks closer than a brother." This scripture highlights the importance of loyalty and steadfastness in relationships—qualities that many individuals with autism naturally embody. By building connections rooted in trust, acceptance, and faith, individuals on the spectrum and their loved ones can experience deep, meaningful relationships that reflect the love of Christ.

1. The Challenges of Navigating Friendships and Relationships on the Spectrum

a. Social Cues and Communication

One of the most significant challenges that individuals on the autism spectrum face in forming friendships and relationships is navigating the complexities of social communication. Neurotypical communication often involves subtle cues—like tone of voice, facial expressions, and body language—that may not be easily interpreted by someone with autism. Understanding when to speak, how to interpret jokes, or when to show empathy can be difficult without clear and direct communication.

For example, while a neurotypical individual might understand that someone crossing their arms during a conversation signals discomfort, an individual with autism might miss or misinterpret this cue. Similarly, sarcasm, which often relies on tone or context, can be confusing. These misunderstandings can create barriers to forming friendships, leading to frustration or withdrawal.

Romans 12:10 advises us to "be devoted to one another in love. Honor one another above yourselves." This verse encourages us to approach relationships with devotion and patience, qualities that are particularly important when navigating the social dynamics between neurotypical individuals and those on the spectrum. By cultivating an environment of understanding and clear communication, we can help individuals on the spectrum engage in relationships that honor their unique way of interacting with the world.

b. Sensory Sensitivities in Social Environments

For many individuals with autism, sensory sensitivities can pose another challenge in social settings. Bright lights, loud noises, crowded spaces, or even certain textures can cause sensory overload, making it difficult to focus on conversations or enjoy social gatherings. This can lead to feelings of isolation or anxiety, as individuals may withdraw from situations that feel overwhelming.

Social events, such as parties or group outings, which are typically seen as opportunities to build friendships, can be particularly challenging for those with sensory sensitivities. The fear of experiencing sensory overload may lead some individuals with autism to avoid these environments altogether, even though they may desire social connection.

1 Corinthians 10:24 teaches us, "No one should seek their own good, but the good of others." This scripture serves as a reminder to consider the needs of others in our relationships. For friends, family members, and communities, creating sensory-friendly environments—such as offering quieter spaces, reducing sensory

input, or allowing time for breaks—can help individuals with autism feel more comfortable and open to building connections.

c. Fear of Rejection

Rejection is a painful experience for anyone, but for individuals on the autism spectrum, the fear of rejection can be especially acute. Social misunderstandings, previous experiences of bullying or exclusion, and a heightened awareness of their differences can make some individuals on the spectrum hesitant to initiate friendships or engage in relationships. The fear of being misunderstood or rejected can lead to social anxiety, making it difficult to pursue meaningful connections.

Matthew 11:28 offers comfort in moments of fear and isolation: "Come to me, all you who are weary and burdened, and I will give you rest." This verse reminds us that, even when we feel rejected by others, God's love is constant and unwavering. Encouraging individuals on the spectrum to lean on their faith and to find strength in God's love can give them the courage to take risks in forming new relationships, knowing that they are valued and accepted by their Creator.

2. The Strengths of Individuals on the Spectrum in Relationships

a. Loyalty and Authenticity

One of the most powerful strengths that individuals on the autism spectrum bring to relationships is their deep sense of loyalty and authenticity. Many individuals with autism approach relationships with sincerity, valuing honesty and straightforward communication. Unlike some neurotypical relationships, which may involve social games or indirect communication, relationships with individuals on the spectrum are often refreshingly genuine. They say what they mean, and they value truth in their interactions.

Proverbs 17:17 says, "A friend loves at all times, and a brother is born for a time of adversity." This scripture speaks to the steadfast love and loyalty that individuals on the spectrum often offer their friends and loved ones. Once a bond is formed, it is likely to be enduring, as individuals with autism tend to be deeply committed to those they care about. Their loyalty is not influenced by social expectations or superficial concerns, but by a genuine desire to connect and support those they love.

This authenticity can be a tremendous asset in relationships, as it fosters trust and openness. Friends and family members can count on the honesty and dependability of their autistic loved ones, knowing that the relationship is built on a solid foundation of truth and care.

b. Unique Perspectives and Insights

Another strength that individuals on the spectrum bring to relationships is their unique perspective on the world. Many autistic individuals have deep interests or passions in specific areas, and their ability to focus intensely on these topics can lead to fascinating conversations and shared experiences. Whether it's an interest in science, history, art, or a particular hobby, these passions can serve as a foundation for meaningful connections with others who share or appreciate their enthusiasm.

1 Peter 4:10 encourages us to "use whatever gift you have received to serve others, as faithful stewards of God's grace in its various forms." This scripture highlights the value of each person's unique gifts, and for individuals with autism, their perspectives and interests are gifts that can enrich their relationships. By sharing

their passions and insights with others, they can forge deep connections based on mutual understanding and appreciation.

Friends and loved ones can support individuals on the spectrum by engaging with their interests, whether that means joining in a favorite activity, listening to them talk about their passion, or simply showing an interest in what excites them. These shared experiences not only strengthen the bond but also help the individual feel seen and valued for who they are.

c. Attention to Detail and Focus in Relationships

Many individuals with autism possess an incredible ability to focus on the people and things that matter most to them. While they may not always express their emotions in traditional ways, their dedication to their friendships and relationships is often profound. They pay close attention to the details that matter—whether it's remembering someone's preferences, showing up in times of need, or being present in important moments.

Philippians 2:4 advises us to "not look to your own interests but each of you to the interests of the others." This verse speaks to the selflessness that individuals on the spectrum often bring to their relationships. Their attention to detail and deep focus on their loved ones can make them incredibly thoughtful and supportive friends, even if their expressions of care differ from neurotypical expectations.

By recognizing and appreciating the unique ways that individuals on the spectrum express their care, friends and family members can build stronger, more supportive relationships. These moments of attentiveness and presence are powerful demonstrations of love and loyalty, creating bonds that are deep and lasting.

3. Building Meaningful Connections: Strategies for Success

a. Fostering Inclusivity and Understanding

For individuals on the autism spectrum, building friendships and relationships often requires an environment of inclusivity, understanding, and respect. Neurotypical individuals play a vital role in creating these environments, by being open to differences in communication, sensory needs, and social interaction styles.

Romans 15:7 calls us to "accept one another, then, just as Christ accepted you, in order to bring praise to God." This scripture underscores the importance of acceptance in building relationships. For individuals on the spectrum, feeling accepted and valued for who they are—without being asked to conform to neurotypical standards—can be the key to forming meaningful connections.

Creating inclusive environments might involve making accommodations for sensory sensitivities, such as providing quieter spaces or offering alternatives to traditional social activities. It also involves clear, direct communication, where expectations and boundaries are openly discussed. By fostering an environment where individuals with autism feel comfortable expressing themselves and their needs, relationships can flourish.

b. Encouraging Open Communication and Empathy

Open communication is essential for building any meaningful relationship, but it is especially important when navigating friendships and relationships with individuals on the spectrum. Because communication styles can differ, it is important to foster an environment where both parties feel comfortable expressing their thoughts, needs, and boundaries.

James 1:19 offers wise counsel on communication: "Everyone should be quick to listen, slow to speak and slow to become angry." This verse reminds us of the importance of listening carefully and responding thoughtfully in our interactions. For neurotypical individuals, this means being patient and understanding when communicating with someone on the spectrum. It also means asking questions, clarifying misunderstandings, and being willing to engage in conversations about preferences and needs.

By creating a culture of open communication and empathy, friends, family members, and partners can build relationships that are grounded in mutual respect and understanding. These relationships, when nurtured with love and patience, can grow into deeply meaningful connections that reflect the love and grace of God.

Conclusion: The Beauty of Connection

Friendships and relationships are a vital part of life, and individuals on the autism spectrum, like everyone else, have a deep need for meaningful connections. While navigating social relationships can present unique challenges for those on the spectrum, it also reveals incredible strengths—loyalty, authenticity, and unique perspectives—that enrich relationships in profound ways.

By fostering inclusive, supportive environments, practicing open communication, and embracing the differences that make each individual special, families, friends, and communities can help individuals on the spectrum build meaningful, lasting connections. Through these relationships, we see a reflection of God's love, a reminder that every person, no matter how they communicate or interact, is deeply valued and worthy of love.

In building these connections, we are reminded of 1 Corinthians 13:4-7, which speaks to the power of love: "Love is patient, love is kind. It does not envy, it does not boast, it is not proud. It does not dishonor others, it is not self-seeking, it is not easily angered, it keeps no record of wrongs. Love does not delight in evil but rejoices with the truth. It always protects, always trusts, always hopes, always perseveres." This passage reminds us that love—rooted in patience, kindness, and understanding—forms the foundation of all meaningful relationships.

With faith, patience, and openness, individuals on the spectrum can experience the beauty of connection, building friendships and relationships that last a lifetime.

Here are some scripture references that align with the theme "Friendships and Relationships: Building Meaningful Connections" for Chapter 1:

1. Proverbs 17:17 (NIV)

"A friend loves at all times, and a brother is born for a time of adversity."
This verse highlights the constancy of true friendship and the deep bonds that can be formed in times of difficulty, emphasizing meaningful and supportive connections.

2. Ecclesiastes 4:9-10 (NIV)

"Two are better than one, because they have a good return for their labor: If either of them falls down, one can help the other up. But pity anyone who falls and has no one to help them up."
This scripture underscores the value of friendship and relationships, emphasizing that we are stronger together, and through meaningful connections, we can support each other in times of need.

3. Proverbs 27:17 (NIV)

"As iron sharpens iron, so one person sharpens another."
This verse speaks to the importance of relationships in refining and strengthening one another, showing how meaningful connections help us grow spiritually and emotionally.

4. John 15:12-13 (NIV)

"My command is this: Love each other as I have loved you. Greater love has no one than this: to lay down one's life for one's friends."
Jesus teaches about sacrificial love, the foundation of deep and meaningful relationships, encouraging us to build connections rooted in love and selflessness.

5. Proverbs 18:24 (NIV)

"One who has unreliable friends soon comes to ruin, but there is a friend who sticks closer than a brother."
This verse highlights the importance of reliability and loyalty in friendships, underscoring the value of meaningful and steadfast relationships.

These scriptures highlight the importance of love, patience, forgiveness, encouragement, and unity in building meaningful friendships and relationships. They underscore the value of nurturing connections that reflect God's love and purpose.

Chapter 7

Autism in Adulthood: Continuing the Journey

"Being confident of this, that he who began a good work in you will carry it on to completion until the day of Christ Jesus."

Philippians 1:6

Introduction: Autism Beyond the Early Years

Autism is frequently discussed in the context of childhood, with much attention focused on early diagnosis, therapies, and developmental milestones. But autism is a lifelong journey, and the experiences of individuals on the spectrum continue to evolve as they transition into adulthood. While the challenges change, so too do the opportunities for growth, self-discovery, and empowerment. The journey of adulthood for those with autism brings new responsibilities, milestones, and pathways, often shaped by the societal expectations of independence, career, and relationships. However, with the right support, understanding, and faith, these challenges can be met with resilience and success.

In this chapter, *Autism in Adulthood: Continuing the Journey*, we will explore the specific challenges that autistic adults face as they navigate life beyond childhood. We will examine how adults on the spectrum adapt to life transitions, including pursuing careers, developing meaningful relationships, and managing their day-to-day lives. Just as important, we will highlight the strengths that autistic adults bring to their communities, families, and workplaces. Through it all, we will turn to scripture for guidance, as the Bible offers profound wisdom on perseverance, faith, and trust in God's plan.

Jeremiah 29:11 serves as a comforting reminder that, "For I know the plans I have for you, declares the Lord, plans for welfare and not for evil, to give you a future and a hope." This scripture speaks directly to the heart of every person's journey, autistic or not, emphasizing that despite life's challenges, there is a divine purpose and future that God has planned for each of us. As autistic adults continue their journey, they do so with the assurance that God is guiding their steps.

1. Navigating Independence: Finding Stability and Self-Advocacy

a. The Challenge of Independence

The transition from childhood to adulthood is often marked by the desire for greater independence—moving out of the family home, managing personal finances, and making long-term decisions about careers and relationships. For autistic adults, this period can be filled with both excitement and anxiety. Many face challenges related to executive functioning, such as planning, organizing, and managing time. Tasks that others may take for granted—budgeting, cooking, or scheduling appointments—can become overwhelming when combined with sensory sensitivities or social anxieties.

Isaiah 41:10 provides comfort for those feeling anxious about this transition: "Fear not, for I am with you; be not dismayed, for I am your God; I will strengthen you, I will help you, I will uphold you with my righteous right hand." This verse reminds autistic individuals that God is always present, offering strength and guidance, even when the path to independence feels difficult.

For many, achieving full independence may involve ongoing support from family members, caregivers, or support services. It's important to acknowledge that independence looks different for everyone and that needing assistance does not diminish one's worth or capabilities. Families and communities can offer practical support—such as helping to set up routines or providing tools to aid in executive functioning—and emotional encouragement, helping their autistic loved ones navigate this period with confidence.

b. Self-Advocacy: Claiming One's Voice

A critical aspect of adulthood for autistic individuals is learning how to advocate for themselves. This includes knowing their rights, communicating their needs, and setting boundaries in personal and professional spaces. Self-advocacy can be empowering, giving individuals the confidence to express themselves and seek out accommodations that allow them to thrive in various environments.

Proverbs 31:8-9 encourages, "Speak up for those who cannot speak for themselves, for the rights of all who are destitute. Speak up and judge fairly; defend the rights of the poor and needy." While this scripture encourages us to advocate for others, it also serves as a reminder of the importance of using our voice to assert our own needs and protect our well-being.

For many autistic adults, learning to self-advocate may involve overcoming feelings of insecurity or fear of rejection. But with faith and the support of loved ones, they can find the courage to stand up for their rights, whether it's in the workplace, in relationships, or in accessing public services. Advocacy organizations and support groups can also play a key role in helping individuals learn how to navigate complex systems and advocate for accommodations that support their unique needs.

2. Career Pathways: Leveraging Strengths in the Workplace

a. Finding the Right Job and Work Environment

Securing meaningful employment is one of the most significant challenges—and opportunities—that autistic adults face. While individuals on the spectrum often possess remarkable strengths, such as attention to detail, persistence, and the ability to focus intensely on tasks, they may encounter obstacles in the hiring process or workplace environment. Traditional job interviews, which often emphasize social skills and unspoken social cues, can be daunting for autistic individuals, leading to misunderstandings or missed opportunities.

Yet, the strengths of autistic individuals align well with certain career paths, particularly those that require precision, creativity, and specialized knowledge. Fields such as technology, art, engineering, and research are often well-suited to individuals on the spectrum, allowing them to leverage their strengths and find fulfillment in their work.

Colossians 3:23-24 provides guidance on approaching work with purpose: "Whatever you do, work heartily, as for the Lord and not for men, knowing that from the Lord you will receive the inheritance as your reward. You are serving the Lord Christ." This scripture reminds us that our work, regardless of its form, is meaningful and part of God's greater plan for us. For autistic adults, finding a job that aligns with their strengths and passions can lead to a sense of fulfillment and purpose.

b. Advocating for Accommodations in the Workplace

For many autistic adults, success in the workplace requires specific accommodations that allow them to manage sensory sensitivities or social challenges. This may include requesting a quieter workspace, using written communication over face-to-face interactions, or having flexible work hours to manage energy levels. While advocating for these accommodations can feel daunting, it's essential for autistic individuals to know their rights and to communicate their needs clearly.

Ephesians 4:29 reminds us of the importance of communication: "Do not let any unwholesome talk come out of your mouths, but only what is helpful for building others up according to their needs, that it may benefit those who listen." Effective communication—done with grace and clarity—is key to building understanding between employees and employers. When employers are open to making accommodations, they not only support their autistic employees but also create a more inclusive and productive work environment for everyone.

3. Relationships and Community in Adulthood

a. Developing Meaningful Relationships

As adults, relationships become a cornerstone of life, offering companionship, support, and a sense of belonging. However, for autistic individuals, forming and maintaining relationships can be challenging due to differences in social communication, sensory sensitivities, or difficulty interpreting nonverbal cues. Romantic relationships, friendships, and professional connections all require navigating a complex social landscape that can feel overwhelming at times.

Yet, autistic adults, like everyone, desire and deserve meaningful relationships. Their authenticity, loyalty, and honesty are qualities that can enrich relationships when both parties are willing to communicate openly and adapt to each other's needs. Autistic individuals often bring a deep sense of commitment and sincerity to their relationships, valuing trust and transparency above all.

Ecclesiastes 4:9-10 reminds us of the power of companionship: "Two are better than one, because they have a good return for their labor: If either of them falls down, one can help the other up. But pity anyone who falls and has no one to help them up." This scripture underscores the importance of relationships in providing mutual support and encouragement, especially during challenging times.

For autistic adults, building relationships may require more intentional effort, such as setting clear boundaries, practicing direct communication, or joining social groups that align with their interests. Support from family members, friends, or therapists can help autistic individuals develop the social skills they need to form and maintain relationships, while also honoring their unique way of engaging with others.

b. The Role of Family and Faith-Based Communities

Family often plays a central role in the lives of autistic adults, providing emotional and practical support as they navigate the challenges of adulthood. For some, family members may serve as advocates, helping to coordinate healthcare, housing, or employment. For others, family serves as a source of unconditional love and acceptance, offering a safe space where they can be themselves without fear of judgment.

The Bible speaks to the importance of family and community in supporting one another. Galatians 6:2 encourages us to "carry each other's burdens, and in this way you will fulfill the law of Christ." This verse highlights the significance of shared support within families and faith-based communities, emphasizing that we are not meant to walk through life's challenges alone.

Faith-based communities can also play a vital role in providing social and spiritual support for autistic adults. Churches, small groups, and religious organizations can create inclusive environments where individuals on the spectrum feel welcomed and valued. By fostering a sense of belonging and offering opportunities for spiritual growth, faith communities can help autistic adults develop meaningful connections that enhance their emotional and spiritual well-being.

4. The Power of Faith in the Adult Journey

a. Trusting in God's Plan

As autistic individuals continue their journey into adulthood, they may encounter moments of uncertainty, frustration, or doubt. Yet, through it all, faith provides a source of strength and reassurance. The Bible teaches us that God has a plan for each of us—a plan that includes both challenges and triumphs, all of which contribute to our growth and purpose.

Jeremiah 29:11 offers a message of hope: "'For I know the plans I have for you,' declares the Lord, 'plans to prosper you and not to harm you, plans to give you hope and a future.'" This scripture reassures autistic individuals that their lives have purpose, even when the path ahead seems unclear. Whether they are facing career challenges, relationship struggles, or personal obstacles, they can trust that God's plan for them is one of hope and growth.

By leaning into their faith, autistic adults can find comfort in knowing that they are not defined by their challenges but by the unique gifts and strengths that God has given them. With God's guidance, they can navigate the complexities of adulthood with confidence, knowing that they are walking in His purpose.

b. Strength Through Perseverance

Perseverance is a key theme in the lives of many autistic adults. Whether it's navigating the workplace, advocating for their needs, or building meaningful relationships, perseverance is required to overcome the obstacles that may arise. But with faith, autistic individuals can find the strength to persevere, even in the face of adversity.

Isaiah 40:31 reminds us that "those who hope in the Lord will renew their strength. They will soar on wings like eagles; they will run and not grow weary, they will walk and not be faint." This scripture speaks to the power of faith in sustaining us through life's challenges. For autistic adults, faith can provide the resilience needed to keep moving forward, even when the journey feels difficult.

By trusting in God's strength, autistic individuals can find peace and hope, knowing that they are not alone in their struggles. With faith as their foundation, they can continue to grow, thrive, and fulfill their unique purpose in life.

Conclusion: Continuing the Journey with Faith and Purpose

Autism in adulthood presents both challenges and opportunities for growth, independence, and fulfillment. While navigating the complexities of careers, relationships, and daily life may require additional support and perseverance, autistic adults possess remarkable strengths that enrich their lives and the lives of those around them. By focusing on their gifts, advocating for their needs, and leaning into their faith, autistic individuals can continue their journey with confidence and purpose.

The journey of adulthood is one of self-discovery and growth, and for autistic individuals, it is a journey that reflects both their unique abilities and their faith in God's plan. As they continue to navigate the challenges and opportunities of adult life, they do so with the assurance that they are walking in God's purpose, guided by His love and grace.

Here are some scripture references that align with the theme "Autism in Adulthood: Continuing the Journey" for Chapter 1:

1. Jeremiah 29:11 (NIV)

"'For I know the plans I have for you,' declares the Lord, 'plans to prosper you and not to harm you, plans to give you hope and a future.'"
God's plan includes hope and a future for every individual, reminding us that the journey continues with His purpose and guidance, even into adulthood.

2. Philippians 1:6 (NIV)

"Being confident of this, that he who began a good work in you will carry it on to completion until the day of Christ Jesus."
God promises to complete the good work He started in each person, signifying that the journey of growth and development, including for those with autism, is ongoing and purposeful.

3. Isaiah 40:31 (NIV)

"But those who hope in the Lord will renew their strength. They will soar on wings like eagles; they will run and not grow weary, they will walk and not be faint."
For adults with autism, the journey can be filled with challenges, but trusting in God brings renewed strength and resilience, allowing them to continue with hope and endurance.

4. Proverbs 16:9 (NIV)

"In their hearts humans plan their course, but the Lord establishes their steps."
Though adults with autism may face unique paths, this verse reminds us that God is guiding their steps and directing their journey, ensuring they are walking in His plan.

5. 2 Corinthians 12:9 (NIV)

"But he said to me, 'My grace is sufficient for you, for my power is made perfect in weakness.' Therefore I will boast all the more gladly about my weaknesses, so that Christ's power may rest on me."
For adults navigating autism, God's grace is sufficient, and His strength is revealed through challenges, showing that their journey is supported by divine power.

These scriptures emphasize God's guidance, strength, and purpose throughout the journey of life, including the unique paths taken by adults with autism. They offer assurance that God is present in every step, providing wisdom, strength, and peace.

Chapter 8

Daily Challenges: Overcoming Obstacles

"Trust in the Lord with all your heart and lean not on your own understanding; in all your ways submit to him, and he will make your paths straight."

Proverbs 3:5-6

Introduction: Embracing Autism's Complexity and Strengths

Autism is a multifaceted experience that affects individuals in unique ways, offering both remarkable strengths and significant challenges. These challenges often present themselves in everyday situations, where sensory sensitivities, social dynamics, communication differences, and routine disruptions can create obstacles that feel overwhelming. Yet, through resilience, the right support, and a deep-rooted faith, individuals on the autism spectrum overcome these obstacles and flourish in their lives. This chapter explores how faith can support the journey of overcoming daily obstacles for those with autism, while highlighting the strengths and gifts that individuals on the spectrum possess.

The Bible offers many insights into overcoming challenges and finding strength through God. One such powerful reminder is found in Isaiah 40:31, which reads, "But those who hope in the Lord will renew their strength. They will soar on wings like eagles; they will run and not grow weary, they will walk and not be faint."

This scripture speaks to the inner strength that can be found in trusting God, reminding individuals with autism, and their families, that even in the face of daily struggles, there is hope and strength through faith.

1. Sensory Overload: Navigating the World of Intense Sensory Input

a. Understanding Sensory Sensitivities

For many individuals on the autism spectrum, the world can be an overwhelming place due to heightened sensitivity to sensory input. Everyday experiences like loud noises, bright lights, strong smells, or the textures of certain fabrics can trigger a sensory overload, leading to discomfort, anxiety, or even meltdowns. These sensory sensitivities can make routine activities like shopping, attending school, or navigating a workplace difficult, as the individual may feel bombarded by stimuli that others don't notice.

Scripture can provide a source of comfort and strength in moments of sensory overload. Psalm 18:2 says, "The Lord is my rock, my fortress and my deliverer; my God is my rock, in whom I take refuge." For individuals with autism, this verse can serve as a reminder that God is a place of refuge, offering calm and security in the midst of overwhelming sensory experiences.

b. Practical Strategies for Managing Sensory Challenges

While sensory overload can be intense, there are practical strategies that can help mitigate its effects. Creating sensory-friendly environments at home or in public spaces, using noise-canceling headphones, sunglasses, or weighted blankets, and allowing for sensory breaks can provide relief. These tools and accommodations help autistic individuals manage their daily environments with greater ease, reducing stress and anxiety.

Loved ones, caregivers, and educators can also play a significant role by being mindful of sensory triggers and helping to create environments that are more comfortable. By advocating for sensory accommodations in schools, workplaces, and public spaces, families and communities can support individuals on the spectrum in overcoming sensory-related challenges.

2. Communication: Finding and Expressing One's Voice

a. Overcoming Communication Barriers

Communication can be one of the most significant daily challenges for individuals with autism. Whether verbal, nonverbal, or somewhere in between, many individuals on the spectrum face difficulties in expressing their thoughts, emotions, and needs in a way that others easily understand. Some may struggle with forming spoken words, while others may have difficulty interpreting nonverbal cues, such as facial expressions or body language. For nonverbal individuals, finding ways to communicate can feel like a constant uphill battle, leaving them feeling isolated or misunderstood.

However, the Bible reminds us that even in moments of struggle, God hears us. Psalm 34:17-18 offers comfort: "The righteous cry out, and the Lord hears them; he delivers them from all their troubles. The Lord is close to the brokenhearted and saves those who are crushed in spirit." For individuals who feel that they cannot communicate in traditional ways, this scripture can serve as a reminder that God hears and understands every heart, even when words cannot be spoken.

b. Tools for Communication and Connection

In overcoming communication challenges, there are many tools and resources available that help individuals with autism express themselves. Augmentative and Alternative Communication (AAC) devices, picture exchange systems, and sign language are just a few methods that allow nonverbal or minimally verbal individuals to find their voice. These tools offer empowerment, helping individuals express their thoughts, preferences, and emotions to others, fostering a sense of autonomy and self-worth.

In addition to technological tools, creating an environment that fosters understanding and patience is crucial. Loved ones can encourage open communication by giving individuals the time and space they need to express themselves, whether through speech, gestures, or assistive devices. This not only helps the individual feel valued but also strengthens relationships.

James 1:19 reminds us, "Everyone should be quick to listen, slow to speak and slow to become angry." This scripture speaks to the importance of listening—something especially relevant when engaging with individuals on the autism spectrum. By practicing patience and being open to nontraditional forms of communication, we can build stronger, more meaningful connections.

3. Routine Disruptions: Managing Change and Uncertainty

a. The Challenge of Changes in Routine

Routine and predictability often bring comfort to individuals with autism. A structured routine helps them navigate the world with a sense of stability and control, making everyday tasks and interactions more manageable. However, unexpected changes or disruptions to these routines—such as a change in schedule, a new environment, or a sudden alteration in plans—can cause significant anxiety and distress. Managing these disruptions is a daily challenge for many autistic individuals.

Ecclesiastes 3:1 reminds us that "there is a time for everything, and a season for every activity under the heavens." While change is a natural part of life, it can feel overwhelming, especially for those who thrive on consistency. This verse offers a sense of peace, reminding us that even in times of uncertainty, God's plan is at work, and each season of life has its purpose.

b. Strategies for Coping with Change

There are ways to help individuals with autism cope with routine disruptions. Visual schedules, social stories, and advanced preparation for any changes can provide a sense of predictability, even when things do not go as planned. Having a "safe space" or calming corner where the individual can retreat when feeling overwhelmed by changes can also be helpful. Additionally, providing consistent reminders or cues about upcoming changes allows the individual to mentally prepare for transitions.

Support systems play a vital role in helping individuals navigate these disruptions. By approaching changes with empathy and understanding, family members, teachers, and caregivers can offer reassurance, helping the individual feel more in control during moments of unpredictability.

Philippians 4:6-7 reminds us not to be anxious about anything: "Do not be anxious about anything, but in every situation, by prayer and petition, with thanksgiving, present your requests to God. And the peace of God, which transcends all understanding, will guard your hearts and your minds in Christ Jesus." This scripture can provide comfort in moments of uncertainty, reminding individuals on the spectrum that God's peace is available to them, even in the face of disruptions.

4. Social Dynamics: Navigating Social Interactions and Relationships

a. The Complexity of Social Interactions

Social interactions are often fraught with unspoken rules, body language, and cultural expectations that can be difficult for individuals with autism to interpret. Understanding sarcasm, humor, or abstract concepts in conversation may be challenging, and navigating group dynamics can feel overwhelming. For some, social anxiety or difficulties in forming relationships may lead to feelings of isolation or exclusion.

Yet, relationships are an essential part of the human experience, and individuals on the spectrum desire meaningful connections just as much as anyone else. The Bible speaks to the importance of companionship in Ecclesiastes 4:9-10: "Two are better than one, because they have a good return for their labor: If either of them falls down, one can help the other up." This scripture underscores the value of friendship and the mutual support that comes from being in relationships with others.

b. Building Meaningful Connections

While social challenges may exist, individuals on the spectrum can and do form deep, meaningful relationships with the right support and understanding. Whether through structured social settings, shared interests, or faith-based communities, autistic individuals can build connections that are fulfilling and genuine. For some, having a trusted friend or mentor who can help interpret social situations or provide guidance can be invaluable.

Loved ones and friends can help by being patient, offering clear communication, and respecting the unique way an autistic individual may engage in social interactions. For example, understanding that an individual may need time to process before responding, or may prefer one-on-one interactions over group settings, can create a more comfortable social environment.

Proverbs 17:17 reminds us that "a friend loves at all times, and a brother is born for a time of adversity." This verse speaks to the power of enduring friendship and reminds us that true friends are those who stand by us, even during difficult moments. By fostering relationships based on patience, acceptance, and love, autistic individuals can overcome social challenges and experience the joy of connection.

5. Overcoming Daily Obstacles with Faith

a. Turning to Scripture for Strength

Scripture offers powerful reminders that no challenge is too great when we lean on God's strength. Whether facing sensory overload, communication barriers, or social difficulties, the Bible reminds us that God is always present, offering guidance and comfort in our times of need.

One particularly powerful verse is found in Isaiah 41:10: "So do not fear, for I am with you; do not be dismayed, for I am your God. I will strengthen you and help you; I will uphold you with my righteous right hand." This scripture is a source of hope for individuals on the spectrum and their families, serving as a reminder that God's strength is available in every circumstance, no matter how challenging it may seem.

b. Building Resilience Through Faith

Resilience is the ability to keep moving forward in the face of adversity, and for individuals on the autism spectrum, this often means finding new ways to navigate daily obstacles with perseverance and creativity. By turning to faith, autistic individuals and their families can find the strength to continue their journey with courage and determination, knowing that they are not alone.

Philippians 4:13 offers encouragement: "I can do all things through Christ who strengthens me." This verse reminds individuals with autism that, with God's help, they have the strength to overcome any challenge, no matter how daunting it may appear. With faith as their foundation, they can meet daily obstacles with confidence, knowing that they are walking a path that has been ordained with purpose.

Conclusion: Rising Above Daily Challenges

The daily challenges faced by individuals on the autism spectrum are real and varied, but they do not define the entirety of their experience. With faith, support, and practical strategies, individuals on the spectrum can rise above these obstacles, embracing their strengths and living lives filled with purpose and meaning. Whether it's navigating sensory overload, finding ways to communicate, managing changes in routine, or building relationships, each challenge is an opportunity for growth, resilience, and connection.

Through it all, the Bible offers wisdom, comfort, and guidance, reminding us that no challenge is too great when we place our trust in God. As individuals on the autism spectrum continue their journey, they can find strength in the knowledge that God is with them, guiding their steps, and offering hope in every season of life.

Here are some scripture references that align with the theme "Daily Challenges: Overcoming Obstacles" for Chapter 1:

1. Philippians 4:13 (NIV)

"I can do all this through him who gives me strength."
This verse reminds us that no matter the obstacles we face, we can overcome them with the strength that God provides.

2. Romans 8:31 (NIV)

"What, then, shall we say in response to these things? If God is for us, who can be against us?"
This passage encourages us to trust that God is with us in every challenge and that nothing can stand in the way of His plan for us.

3. James 1:2-4 (NIV)

"Consider it pure joy, my brothers and sisters, whenever you face trials of many kinds, because you know that the testing of your faith produces perseverance. Let perseverance finish its work so that you may be mature and complete, not lacking anything."
Trials and challenges serve to build perseverance and maturity, encouraging us to see obstacles as opportunities for growth.

4. Isaiah 41:10 (NIV)

"So do not fear, for I am with you; do not be dismayed, for I am your God. I will strengthen you and help you; I will uphold you with my righteous right hand."

God promises His presence, strength, and support in overcoming challenges, encouraging us not to fear but to trust in His help.

5. 2 Corinthians 12:9-10 (NIV)

"But he said to me, 'My grace is sufficient for you, for my power is made perfect in weakness.' Therefore I will boast all the more gladly about my weaknesses, so that Christ's power may rest on me."
God's grace is enough to help us through our struggles, and His power is demonstrated in our weaknesses, reminding us that obstacles are opportunities to rely on His strength.

6. Psalm 34:17 (NIV)

"The righteous cry out, and the Lord hears them; he delivers them from all their troubles."
God is attentive to our cries for help, offering deliverance from the challenges we face daily.

These scriptures offer encouragement, strength, and reassurance that with God's help, we can overcome the obstacles we face daily. Each verse highlights God's presence, power, and promises, which sustain us in times of difficulty.

Chapter 9
The Spectrum of Perception: Understanding Autism

"Yet you, Lord, are our Father. We are the clay, you are the potter; we are all the work of your hand."

Isaiah 64:8

Introduction: The Diversity of the Autism Spectrum

Autism Spectrum Disorder (ASD) is often described as a "spectrum" because no two individuals with autism are exactly alike. The spectrum reflects the wide range of abilities, challenges, and experiences that people on the autism spectrum possess. Some individuals may have profound challenges with communication, social interaction, and sensory processing, while others may excel in certain areas, such as attention to detail, creativity, or problem-solving. The spectrum is vast and varied, and to understand autism fully, we must embrace the complexity and beauty of these differences.

In this chapter, *The Spectrum of Perception: Understanding Autism*, we will explore the many ways autism affects perception, behavior, and interaction with the world. We will discuss the challenges individuals on the spectrum face—such as sensory sensitivities, communication barriers, and social difficulties—while also highlighting the strengths they possess, such as creativity, honesty, and unique problem-solving abilities. Throughout this chapter, we will also turn to scripture to provide support and guidance, recognizing the power of faith in helping individuals on the spectrum, and their families, overcome obstacles and embrace their unique identities.

Psalm 139:14 declares, "I praise you because I am fearfully and wonderfully made; your works are wonderful, I know that full well." This verse serves as a reminder that each individual, including those on the autism spectrum, is created by God with purpose and intention. Autism, with all its complexities, is part of the diverse and beautiful tapestry of God's creation, and understanding the spectrum means embracing the strengths and challenges that come with it.

1. Perception and Sensory Sensitivities: A Different Experience of the World

a. Sensory Overload and Sensory Seeking

One of the most common characteristics of autism is sensory sensitivity. For many individuals on the spectrum, the world can feel overwhelming due to heightened sensitivities to sound, light, touch, smell, and even taste. Everyday environments, such as busy shopping malls, loud classrooms, or even bright fluorescent lights, can become sources of intense discomfort or anxiety. Sensory overload occurs when too much sensory input floods the nervous system, making it difficult for the individual to process the information.

Conversely, some individuals with autism may be hyposensitive to sensory input, meaning they seek out more intense stimuli to feel grounded or comfortable. This may manifest in behaviors such as hand-flapping, rocking, or spinning, often referred to as "stimming" (self-stimulatory behavior), which helps regulate sensory experiences.

The Bible provides comfort in moments of overwhelm. Psalm 61:2 says, "From the ends of the earth I call to you, I call as my heart grows faint; lead me to the rock that is higher than I." This scripture reminds us that when the sensory world feels chaotic and overpowering, God is our refuge and strength. He provides a place of calm in the storm, helping individuals on the spectrum find peace in the midst of sensory challenges.

b. Practical Strategies for Managing Sensory Sensitivities

Managing sensory sensitivities is essential for individuals on the spectrum to navigate daily life more comfortably. Creating sensory-friendly environments at home, school, and work can greatly improve their well-being. Some practical strategies include:

Noise-canceling headphones to reduce auditory overload.
Dimming lights or using natural lighting to prevent visual overstimulation.
Weighted blankets or fidget toys to provide sensory input and comfort.
Quiet spaces where individuals can retreat when feeling overwhelmed.

By incorporating these accommodations into their daily routines, individuals with autism can better manage their sensory experiences and reduce anxiety. Family members, educators, and employers can support these efforts by being mindful of sensory triggers and creating environments that are conducive to sensory regulation.

Romans 12:10 encourages us to "be devoted to one another in love. Honor one another above yourselves." This scripture speaks to the importance of empathy and understanding in our relationships with others. By honoring the sensory needs of individuals on the spectrum, we demonstrate love and care, helping them thrive in environments that respect their unique experiences.

2. Communication: A Spectrum of Expression

a. Verbal and Nonverbal Communication Differences

Communication is another area where individuals with autism often experience significant differences. Some individuals with autism are nonverbal or minimally verbal, relying on alternative forms of communication such as Augmentative and Alternative Communication (AAC) devices, picture exchange systems, or sign language to express themselves. Others may develop spoken language but struggle with the social aspects of communication, such as understanding sarcasm, tone of voice, or body language.

For nonverbal individuals, the challenge of expressing their thoughts, emotions, and needs in a world that prioritizes verbal communication can lead to frustration and isolation. However, it is important to remember that nonverbal does not mean non-communicative. Many nonverbal individuals have rich inner lives and profound thoughts that may be expressed through other means, such as art, writing, or behavior.

Romans 8:26 offers reassurance in times of communication struggles: "In the same way, the Spirit helps us in our weakness. We do not know what we ought to pray for, but the Spirit himself intercedes for us through wordless groans." This verse reminds us that God understands the heart, even when we cannot find the words to express ourselves. For individuals with autism, this is a comforting reminder that their inner thoughts and feelings are known and understood by God, even when they struggle to communicate with others.

b. Supporting Alternative Communication Methods

Supporting communication for individuals on the spectrum means embracing a variety of tools and strategies that allow them to express themselves in ways that work best for them. AAC devices, visual schedules, and social stories can help individuals communicate more effectively, fostering independence and reducing frustration.

It is important for family members, teachers, and caregivers to learn and use these communication tools, ensuring that individuals with autism feel heard and understood. Patience and empathy are key, as it may take time for autistic individuals to communicate their thoughts or needs, but the effort to connect is always worthwhile.

Proverbs 18:21 reminds us, "The tongue has the power of life and death, and those who love it will eat its fruit." This scripture highlights the power of communication, both verbal and nonverbal, in building relationships and understanding. By valuing alternative forms of communication, we affirm the dignity and worth of every individual, regardless of how they express themselves.

3. Social Interaction: Navigating the Complexities of Connection

a. The Challenges of Social Interaction

Social interaction can be particularly challenging for individuals with autism, especially when it comes to interpreting social cues, understanding unspoken rules, or navigating group dynamics. Many individuals on the spectrum may struggle with eye contact, facial expressions, or recognizing subtle changes in tone that signal sarcasm or humor. As a result, they may feel out of sync in social settings, leading to social anxiety or withdrawal.

However, it is important to recognize that individuals with autism often have a strong desire for connection and friendship. While their approach to social interaction may be different, their capacity for deep, meaningful relationships is profound. Autistic individuals often value honesty, loyalty, and authenticity in their relationships, and once bonds are formed, they are often long-lasting and genuine.

Ecclesiastes 4:9-10 reminds us of the importance of companionship: "Two are better than one, because they have a good return for their labor: If either of them falls down, one can help the other up." This scripture emphasizes the value of relationships and mutual support, especially during times of difficulty. For individuals with autism, finding friends who understand and accept their unique way of interacting can provide a source of strength and encouragement.

b. Building Meaningful Relationships

Building meaningful relationships with individuals on the autism spectrum requires patience, understanding, and a willingness to engage in different ways of connecting. Some individuals on the spectrum may prefer one-on-one interactions over group settings, while others may need clear and direct communication to feel comfortable. Respecting these preferences and being mindful of sensory sensitivities can help create an environment where autistic individuals feel valued and accepted.

For family members, friends, and caregivers, it is essential to offer support in social settings by providing structure and guidance when needed. This may include helping the individual navigate conversations, explaining social cues, or offering reassurance in moments of uncertainty.

Proverbs 17:17 reminds us, "A friend loves at all times, and a brother is born for a time of adversity." This verse speaks to the power of friendship, especially in moments of challenge. By being a source of support and understanding, we can help individuals with autism build lasting and meaningful relationships that enrich their lives.

4. Focusing on Strengths: Embracing the Gifts of Autism

a. Attention to Detail and Deep Focus

One of the strengths that many individuals with autism possess is the ability to focus deeply on specific interests or topics. This intense focus, often referred to as "special interests," can lead to a wealth of knowledge and expertise in particular areas, such as science, technology, art, or history. Autistic individuals often have a keen attention to detail, noticing patterns and nuances that others may overlook.

While society sometimes views these focused interests as "obsessions" or "quirks," it is important to recognize them as gifts. Many autistic individuals use their deep focus and attention to detail to solve complex problems, create innovative art, or excel in academic or professional settings.

1 Peter 4:10 encourages us to use our gifts to serve others: "Each of you should use whatever gift you have received to serve others, as faithful stewards of God's grace in its various forms." This scripture reminds us that the strengths and talents of individuals with autism are part of God's design, meant to be shared with the world. By embracing and nurturing these gifts, we allow autistic individuals to contribute in meaningful ways to their communities.

b. Creativity, Innovation, and Problem-Solving

Autistic individuals often bring a fresh perspective to problem-solving and creativity. Their ability to think outside the box, coupled with their unique way of processing information, allows them to approach challenges with innovative solutions. Many individuals on the spectrum excel in fields that require creative thinking, such as technology, engineering, art, and music.

For families and educators, it is essential to provide opportunities for autistic individuals to explore and develop their creative talents. Encouraging their interests and offering outlets for expression can help build confidence and foster a sense of accomplishment.

Philippians 4:13 offers a message of empowerment: "I can do all things through Christ who strengthens me." This verse speaks to the potential that lies within each individual, regardless of their challenges. For individuals with autism, it is a reminder that their unique gifts and strengths, when combined with faith, can lead to great accomplishments.

Conclusion: Embracing the Full Spectrum of Autism

Autism is a spectrum that encompasses a wide range of experiences, abilities, and challenges. Understanding autism requires us to look beyond the labels and embrace the diversity of perception, communication, and interaction that individuals on the spectrum bring to the world. While challenges such as sensory overload, communication barriers, and social difficulties are real, they are balanced by strengths such as creativity, attention to detail, and deep focus.

As we seek to understand autism, we must turn to scripture for guidance and support. The Bible teaches us that every person is "fearfully and wonderfully made" (Psalm 139:14), a reminder that each individual, regardless of their neurotype, has been created with purpose and love. By embracing the full spectrum of autism, we not only support individuals in overcoming their challenges but also celebrate the gifts they bring to the world.

In understanding autism, we recognize that each person's journey is unique, shaped by their strengths, challenges, and experiences. Through faith, love, and understanding, we can create a world where individuals with autism are valued, supported, and empowered to live lives of purpose and fulfillment.

Here are some scripture references that align with the theme "The Spectrum of Perception: Understanding Autism" for Chapter 1:

1. Psalm 139:13-14 (NIV)

"For you created my inmost being; you knit me together in my mother's womb. I praise you because I am fearfully and wonderfully made; your works are wonderful, I know that full well."
This passage emphasizes the uniqueness of every individual, including those with autism, reminding us that each person is wonderfully made by God's hand.

2. 1 Corinthians 12:18-20 (NIV)

"But in fact God has placed the parts in the body, every one of them, just as he wanted them to be. If they were all one part, where would the body be? As it is, there are many parts, but one body."
This verse reminds us that everyone has a unique role to play in God's creation, and the diversity in perception, including autism, contributes to the richness of the body of Christ.

3. Jeremiah 1:5 (NIV)

"Before I formed you in the womb I knew you, before you were born I set you apart; I appointed you as a prophet to the nations."
God knows each person intimately and has a purpose for them, even before they are born. This verse affirms the value and purpose of every person, including those with autism.

4. Isaiah 64:8 (NIV)

"Yet you, Lord, are our Father. We are the clay, you are the potter; we are all the work of your hand."
This verse speaks to the idea that God carefully shapes each of us according to His design, including our unique perspectives and abilities.

5. 1 Samuel 16:7 (NIV)

"But the Lord said to Samuel, 'Do not consider his appearance or his height, for I have rejected him. The Lord does not look at the things people look at. People look at the outward appearance, but the Lord looks at the heart.'"
God sees beyond external appearances and values the heart, encouraging us to look beyond surface perceptions when understanding autism.

These scriptures reflect the uniqueness and value of every person, including those with autism, and emphasize God's purpose, love, and care for all of His creation.

Chapter 10

Workplace Inclusion: Harnessing Potential

"Whatever you do, work at it with all your heart, as working for the Lord, not for human masters, since you know that you will receive an inheritance from the Lord as a reward. It is the Lord Christ you are serving."

Colossians 3:23-24

Introduction: The Power of Inclusion and Diversity in the Workplace

Workplace inclusion is more than just a legal or ethical responsibility—it's an opportunity to tap into the diverse talents and abilities of individuals, particularly those on the autism spectrum. Autism is often misunderstood in professional environments, where the challenges that individuals face may be seen as barriers to effective participation. However, when properly understood and supported, autistic individuals bring unique strengths to the workplace, including attention to detail, creativity, and problem-solving abilities that are unparalleled.

In this chapter, *Workplace Inclusion: Harnessing Potential*, we will explore how employers can create inclusive environments that allow individuals on the autism spectrum to thrive. We will discuss the barriers that exist in traditional workplace settings and offer practical strategies for overcoming these obstacles. Moreover, we will look at the strengths autistic individuals bring to their workplaces and how these strengths can be leveraged to benefit the entire organization. Throughout this chapter, we will also turn to scripture for guidance and wisdom, recognizing the role faith plays in fostering understanding, compassion, and inclusion.

Scripture reminds us of the importance of inclusion and the value of each individual. In 1 Corinthians 12:12, we read, "Just as a body, though one, has many parts, but all its many parts form one body, so it is with Christ." This verse beautifully illustrates that every person—regardless of their abilities—has a role to play in the larger community. In the workplace, individuals on the autism spectrum are vital members of the body, each bringing unique gifts that, when properly supported, contribute to the health and success of the whole.

1. The Strengths of Individuals on the Autism Spectrum

a. Attention to Detail and Deep Focus

One of the most widely recognized strengths of individuals with autism is their ability to focus deeply on tasks, particularly those involving patterns, details, or structured processes. Many autistic individuals excel in fields that require precision and attention to detail, such as data analysis, coding, engineering, scientific research, and quality assurance. Their ability to stay focused on a task, sometimes for extended periods, allows them to identify patterns or errors that might be overlooked by others.

This attention to detail is not just a skill—it is a gift. Autistic individuals often have an innate ability to see things that others may miss, and this capability is an invaluable asset in industries where accuracy is crucial.

Proverbs 22:29 speaks to the value of diligence and skill: "Do you see someone skilled in their work? They will serve before kings; they will not serve before officials of low rank." This scripture highlights the importance of skill and dedication in one's work, a characteristic that many autistic individuals possess in abundance. Employers who recognize and value this strength can harness it to improve productivity and innovation in their workplaces.

b. Creativity and Innovation

Another strength often seen in autistic individuals is their creativity and ability to think outside the box. Autistic individuals are known for approaching problems from unique angles, bringing fresh perspectives to challenges that require creative solutions. This ability to innovate can be particularly valuable in fields such as technology, design, and engineering, where creative thinking often leads to breakthroughs and advancements.

Because autistic individuals process information differently, they may be able to solve problems that others struggle with by applying their unique thought processes and deep understanding of a particular subject. Their creativity is often reflected in their work, whether through innovative designs, inventive solutions, or novel approaches to everyday tasks.

In Exodus 35:35, we are reminded of the divine nature of creativity: "He has filled them with skill to do all kinds of work as engravers, designers, embroiderers… and all of them skilled workers and designers." This scripture affirms that creativity is a gift from God, and when nurtured, it can lead to remarkable achievements. Employers should embrace the creativity of autistic individuals, giving them opportunities to apply their innovative ideas to workplace challenges.

c. Integrity and Loyalty

Autistic individuals are often characterized by their strong sense of loyalty and integrity. Many individuals on the spectrum value honesty, transparency, and consistency in their interactions. This means that, once given a task, they are likely to complete it with accuracy and dedication. Their work ethic is often driven by a desire to do the job well, rather than focusing on superficial workplace politics or social expectations.

This quality of integrity makes autistic individuals particularly valuable in roles that require trust and reliability. Employers often find that autistic employees are not only hardworking but also committed to their roles, often going above and beyond to ensure that tasks are completed to a high standard.

Colossians 3:23 reminds us of the importance of working with integrity: "Whatever you do, work at it with all your heart, as working for the Lord, not for human masters." This scripture encourages a mindset of dedication and integrity in one's work, which aligns with the natural tendencies of many autistic individuals. Their commitment to doing their work well and their focus on accuracy make them invaluable contributors to any organization.

2. Overcoming Barriers: Creating an Inclusive Workplace

a. Breaking Down Stereotypes and Misconceptions

One of the most significant barriers to workplace inclusion for individuals with autism is the persistence of stereotypes and misconceptions. Employers may assume that individuals with autism are incapable of handling certain roles or responsibilities due to their differences in communication or social interaction. These misconceptions can lead to a lack of opportunities for autistic individuals and prevent organizations from benefiting from their unique strengths.

It is essential to move beyond these stereotypes and recognize that autism does not define an individual's capabilities. Employers must educate themselves and their teams about the reality of autism and the diversity of experiences within the spectrum. Each autistic individual is unique, and it is important to focus on their abilities rather than making assumptions based on misconceptions.

Romans 12:2 encourages us to "be transformed by the renewing of your mind." This scripture calls for an openness to new ways of thinking, which can be applied to breaking down the barriers of stereotypes and biases. By renewing our perspectives on autism and embracing neurodiversity, we can foster more inclusive workplaces that value diversity in all its forms.

b. Providing Practical Accommodations

Creating an inclusive workplace often requires providing practical accommodations that support the unique needs of autistic individuals. These accommodations can range from sensory adjustments to communication support. For example, some autistic individuals may be sensitive to noise or bright lights and would benefit from noise-canceling headphones, dimmer lighting, or the option to work in a quieter environment. Others may need structured routines, clear instructions, or visual supports to help them process information more effectively.

Flexibility is also crucial in creating an inclusive workplace. Allowing employees to adjust their work hours or work remotely can help reduce anxiety and sensory overload. Additionally, recognizing that traditional job interviews may not accurately reflect an autistic individual's abilities is key. Offering alternative assessments, such as work trials or project-based evaluations, can provide a more accurate picture of a candidate's skills and potential.

1 Corinthians 12:22-23 reminds us, "On the contrary, those parts of the body that seem to be weaker are indispensable, and the parts that we think are less honorable we treat with special honor." This scripture emphasizes the importance of accommodating and honoring those who may have different needs or abilities. By providing accommodations, employers not only support their autistic employees but also demonstrate that every team member is valued and respected.

c. Clear Communication and Setting Expectations

For many autistic individuals, communication differences can pose a challenge in the workplace, particularly when unspoken social rules or ambiguous instructions are involved. Employers can support their autistic employees by providing clear, direct communication and setting explicit expectations for tasks and responsibilities. This might involve giving instructions in writing, breaking down tasks into smaller steps, or providing visual aids to enhance understanding.

Clear communication benefits all employees, not just those with autism, as it fosters transparency and reduces misunderstandings. By creating a workplace culture where expectations are communicated clearly and consistently, employers can help their autistic employees feel more confident and empowered in their roles.

James 1:19 offers wisdom in communication: "Everyone should be quick to listen, slow to speak and slow to become angry." This scripture encourages us to practice patience and attentiveness in our interactions, which is essential in creating a workplace where all employees, including those on the spectrum, feel heard and understood.

3. Building a Culture of Inclusion: Fostering Support and Collaboration

a. Peer Support and Mentorship

One of the most effective ways to foster workplace inclusion for autistic individuals is through peer support and mentorship programs. Having a supportive colleague or mentor who can provide guidance, offer feedback, and serve as a point of contact can make a significant difference in helping autistic employees navigate the workplace. Mentorship programs not only benefit the mentee but also promote a culture of collaboration and mutual understanding.

A supportive peer or mentor can help autistic employees acclimate to the workplace, navigate social dynamics, and gain confidence in their abilities. In turn, this support fosters stronger workplace relationships and contributes to a more inclusive and cohesive team environment.

Ecclesiastes 4:9-10 speaks to the value of support in relationships: "Two are better than one, because they have a good return for their labor: If either of them falls down, one can help the other up." This verse highlights the importance of teamwork and mutual support, which are essential components of an inclusive workplace. By fostering an environment where employees support one another, organizations can create a stronger, more cohesive team that values the contributions of every member.

b. Promoting Awareness and Education

Inclusion is not just about making accommodations—it's about building a culture of understanding and acceptance. Employers can promote awareness of autism in the workplace by offering training sessions, workshops, or resources that help staff members learn about neurodiversity. When colleagues understand the strengths and challenges that come with autism, they are better equipped to work alongside their autistic peers in a supportive and inclusive manner.

Romans 14:13 calls for us to "make up your mind not to put any stumbling block or obstacle in the way of a brother or sister." This scripture encourages us to be mindful of the ways we interact with others, ensuring that we do not create unnecessary barriers or challenges. By promoting awareness and understanding of autism, employers can remove obstacles that may prevent autistic individuals from fully participating in the workplace.

c. Celebrating Neurodiversity

Fostering workplace inclusion means celebrating neurodiversity as a strength rather than a limitation. Neurodiverse individuals bring a range of perspectives, skills, and talents that can enhance creativity, problem-solving, and innovation within an organization. By embracing neurodiversity, employers not only create a more inclusive environment but also benefit from the unique contributions of their autistic employees.

1 Peter 4:10 reminds us, "Each of you should use whatever gift you have received to serve others, as faithful stewards of God's grace in its various forms." This scripture emphasizes the value of each person's unique gifts, and for autistic individuals, their strengths are part of the diversity that enriches the workplace. By celebrating

neurodiversity, employers create a culture where differences are not only accepted but appreciated.

Conclusion: The Future of Workplace Inclusion

Creating an inclusive workplace is not just about meeting legal requirements or accommodating differences; it's about recognizing and celebrating the unique strengths that individuals on the autism spectrum bring to the table. By providing practical accommodations, clear communication, and a supportive culture, employers can harness the potential of their autistic employees, contributing to the overall success of the organization.

The Bible teaches us the importance of valuing every individual and creating environments where everyone can contribute their gifts and talents. As 1 Corinthians 12:12 reminds us, "Just as a body, though one, has many parts, but all its many parts form one body," each person is a vital part of the whole. By embracing the strengths of autistic individuals, we create a more diverse, innovative, and compassionate workplace—one that reflects the power of inclusion and the grace of God's design.

Through faith, compassion, and practical action, we can build workplaces that not only accommodate but celebrate neurodiversity, allowing every individual to fulfill their God-given potential.

Here are some scripture references that align with the theme "Workplace Inclusion: Harnessing Potential" for Chapter 1:

1. Colossians 3:23-24 (NIV)

"Whatever you do, work at it with all your heart, as working for the Lord, not for human masters, since you know that you will receive an inheritance from the Lord as a reward. It is the Lord Christ you are serving."
This verse encourages everyone to work wholeheartedly, reminding us that every person's work is valuable, regardless of differences or abilities, and should be done as unto the Lord.

2. 1 Corinthians 12:12-14 (NIV)

"Just as a body, though one, has many parts, but all its many parts form one body, so it is with Christ. For we were all baptized by one Spirit so as to form one body—whether Jews or Gentiles, slave or free—and we were all given the one Spirit to drink. Even so the body is not made up of one part but of many."
This passage reminds us of the diversity in the body of Christ and the importance of every member's contribution. In the workplace, inclusion ensures that everyone's unique potential can be harnessed for the greater good.

3. Romans 12:4-6 (NIV)

"For just as each of us has one body with many members, and these members do not all have the same function, so in Christ we, though many, form one body, and each member belongs to all the others. We have different gifts, according to the grace given to each of us."
This verse speaks to the unique gifts and talents that each individual brings to the workplace, encouraging inclusion by acknowledging the diversity of skills and roles.

4. Galatians 3:28 (NIV)

"There is neither Jew nor Gentile, neither slave nor free, nor is there male and female, for you are all one in Christ Jesus."

This scripture emphasizes unity and equality in Christ, which can be reflected in the workplace by ensuring that everyone, regardless of background or ability, has the opportunity to contribute and succeed.

5. James 2:1-4 (NIV)

"My brothers and sisters, believers in our glorious Lord Jesus Christ must not show favoritism. Suppose a man comes into your meeting wearing a gold ring and fine clothes, and a poor man in filthy old clothes also comes in. If you show special attention to the man wearing fine clothes and say, 'Here's a good seat for you,' but say to the poor man, 'You stand there' or 'Sit on the floor by my feet,' have you not discriminated among yourselves and become judges with evil thoughts?"
This passage warns against favoritism and discrimination, urging fairness and equal treatment in all settings, including the workplace, where every person's potential should be harnessed regardless of appearance or status.

These scriptures emphasize the importance of recognizing the unique gifts and talents that everyone brings to the workplace and fostering an inclusive environment where those talents can be fully harnessed for the benefit of all.

Chapter 11

Self-Advocacy and Empowerment: Voices Rising

"Have I not commanded you? Be strong and courageous. Do not be afraid; do not be discouraged, for the Lord your God will be with you wherever you go."

Joshua 1:9

Introduction: The Rise of Autistic Voices

Self-advocacy is the cornerstone of empowerment, especially for individuals on the autism spectrum. Historically, those with autism have often been spoken *for* rather than *with*, leading to a narrative where their voices were rarely heard. Now, more than ever, autistic individuals are stepping forward, challenging societal expectations, and advocating for their rights, needs, and unique strengths. They are moving beyond the labels that define them and claiming their place as powerful advocates for themselves and their communities.

This chapter, *Self-Advocacy and Empowerment: Voices Rising*, delves into the importance of self-advocacy for autistic individuals. It explores the challenges they face, the strategies they can employ, and the ultimate strength they gain by reclaiming their voice. By looking to scripture, we will also reflect on the role of faith in empowering self-advocacy and how God calls each of us to rise with confidence, understanding that we are fearfully and wonderfully made in His image.

Romans 8:37 reminds us, " in all these things we are more than conquerors through him who loved us." This verse speaks to the power that lies within each individual, especially those who have been marginalized or overlooked. Through faith and the act of self-advocacy, autistic individuals can rise above the barriers placed before them, harnessing their inner strength and the gifts that God has given them.

1. Understanding Self-Advocacy: What It Means for Autistic Individuals

a. The Importance of Finding Your Voice

Self-advocacy is the ability to speak up for oneself, express one's needs, and take control of one's life. For individuals on the autism spectrum, this involves recognizing personal strengths and challenges, understanding rights and responsibilities, and communicating those needs to others—whether in personal relationships, educational settings, or workplaces. Many autistic individuals grow up in environments where they are either misunderstood or spoken over. As they mature, learning to self-advocate becomes a critical tool for gaining independence and living authentically.

The challenges of self-advocacy for autistic individuals are often rooted in differences in communication styles and sensory processing. For example, some autistic individuals may find it difficult to communicate verbally and may rely on alternative communication methods like writing or assistive technology. Others may have sensory sensitivities that make certain environments overwhelming, and advocating for accommodations in these situations can be both daunting and necessary.

James 1:19 offers wisdom about communication: "Everyone should be quick to listen, slow to speak and slow to become angry." This reminds us that self-advocacy involves both speaking up and ensuring that others are willing to listen. As autistic individuals learn to advocate for themselves, they also help those around them understand that communication and needs come in many forms. The key to empowerment is ensuring that these voices are heard with patience, respect, and understanding.

b. The Role of Faith in Empowering Self-Advocacy

For many autistic individuals, self-advocacy can feel overwhelming, especially when they face misunderstanding or discrimination. However, faith can provide the foundation for courage and resilience. The Bible frequently encourages believers to be strong and courageous, to trust in God's plan, and to remember that each person is created with a purpose.

Isaiah 41:10 reassures us, "So do not fear, for I am with you; do not be dismayed, for I am your God. I will strengthen you and help you; I will uphold you with my righteous right hand." For autistic individuals, this verse serves as a reminder that they are never alone in their journey of self-advocacy. God walks with them, providing strength and guidance as they seek to express their needs and claim their space in the world.

Faith also reminds autistic individuals that their unique gifts are part of God's design. Ephesians 2:10 says, "For we are God's handiwork, created in Christ Jesus to do good works, which God prepared in advance for us to do." Self-advocacy is not just about claiming rights; it is about recognizing that each person, including those with autism, has a unique and God-given contribution to make to the world. By advocating for their needs and embracing their strengths, autistic individuals live out the purpose that God has set for them.

2. The Challenges of Self-Advocacy for Autistic Individuals

a. Misunderstandings and Communication Barriers

One of the biggest obstacles to self-advocacy for autistic individuals is the way they are often misunderstood by neurotypical society. Communication differences, such as difficulty interpreting social cues, or reliance on nonverbal methods of communication, can make it challenging for autistic individuals to express their needs effectively. In some cases, their directness in communication may be mistaken for rudeness, or their difficulty in verbal expression might be misinterpreted as disinterest or lack of ability.

This misunderstanding extends to the way others perceive autistic behavior. For instance, stimming (self-stimulatory behavior) is often misunderstood by neurotypical people as odd or disruptive, when in fact it serves as a crucial tool for self-regulation and sensory management. When autistic individuals self-advocate for their need to stim or request specific accommodations like sensory breaks, they may encounter resistance from those who do not fully understand the purpose behind these requests.

In Mark 7:37, the people of Jesus' time marveled at His ability to "do all things well," particularly in helping those who were marginalized by society. This same spirit of understanding is needed in today's world, where individuals with different needs, such as those with autism, require patience and open-mindedness from their communities. Just as Christ reached out to those on the fringes, society must reach out and listen to autistic voices without judgment or misunderstanding.

b. Navigating Power Dynamics

For many autistic individuals, self-advocacy means challenging existing power structures in schools, workplaces, and even family dynamics. They may need to assert their needs to people who hold authority, such as teachers, employers, or medical professionals. This can be a daunting task, especially in environments where autistic voices have historically been silenced or dismissed.

When advocating for accommodations, autistic individuals may face barriers such as skepticism or outright denial of their needs. They may worry about being labeled as "difficult" or fear retaliation for requesting adjustments that allow them to thrive. These power dynamics can make self-advocacy feel like an uphill battle, especially when individuals are advocating for basic needs like sensory accommodations, communication aids, or changes in routine.

Proverbs 31:8-9 encourages us to "speak up for those who cannot speak for themselves, for the rights of all who are destitute. Speak up and judge fairly; defend the rights of the poor and needy." This scripture calls for justice and fairness, reminding us that self-advocacy is a righteous act, and those who advocate for themselves or others are participating in a greater pursuit of equity. Autistic individuals should find strength in knowing that their advocacy is aligned with biblical principles of justice and fairness.

3. Building Self-Advocacy Skills: Practical Strategies for Empowerment

a. Knowing Your Rights and Needs

The first step in becoming an effective self-advocate is understanding your rights and needs. Whether in school, at work, or in personal relationships, autistic individuals have the right to ask for accommodations that allow them to participate fully and succeed. In educational settings, this might mean requesting extra time on tests or access to sensory-friendly environments. In the workplace, it could involve asking for flexible work hours or noise-reducing headphones to manage sensory sensitivities.

Knowing what accommodations are available is key. For example, under laws like the Americans with Disabilities Act (ADA) or the Individuals with Disabilities Education Act (IDEA), autistic individuals are entitled to reasonable accommodations in both school and work settings. Educating oneself on these rights is a critical part of self-advocacy, as it empowers individuals to make informed requests and stand up for their legal entitlements.

Philippians 4:6 offers guidance on how to approach self-advocacy with faith: "Do not be anxious about anything, but in every situation, by prayer and petition, with thanksgiving, present your requests to God." This verse encourages autistic individuals to bring their needs to God in prayer, trusting that He will provide guidance and peace. Just as we present our requests to God, we can confidently present our requests to those in authority, knowing that we are advocating for our well-being.

b. Developing Communication Strategies

Effective communication is central to self-advocacy, but for many autistic individuals, it can be one of the most challenging aspects of the process. Developing communication strategies that work for each individual is essential. For some, this might mean practicing clear and direct verbal communication, while for others, it might involve using written communication, visual aids, or assistive technology.

Role-playing self-advocacy scenarios with a trusted friend or family member can help autistic individuals prepare for real-world advocacy situations. Practicing how to request accommodations, explain one's needs, or navigate conflict in a controlled environment can build confidence and reduce anxiety. Additionally, having a support person or ally present during advocacy situations can provide extra reassurance and help bridge communication gaps.

Colossians 4:6 provides insight into how we can approach communication: "Let your conversation be always full of grace, seasoned with salt, so that you may know how to answer everyone." This scripture emphasizes the importance of grace in communication. For autistic individuals, practicing self-advocacy with grace—both toward themselves and others—helps to ensure that their needs are heard and understood without unnecessary conflict or tension.

4. Empowerment Through Community: Strength in Numbers

a. The Power of Allies and Support Networks

Self-advocacy is often strongest when supported by a network of allies. For autistic individuals, building a support network of family, friends, coworkers, and advocates can provide the encouragement and assistance needed to navigate self-advocacy challenges. These allies can help amplify the individual's voice, offering additional support in situations where self-advocacy alone may not be enough.

In workplaces, having an ally who understands the individual's needs and can help advocate for accommodations is invaluable. In educational settings, teachers, guidance counselors, and special education coordinators can serve as allies who ensure that autistic students receive the resources and support they need. Outside of formal environments, family members and friends can also play a key role in empowering autistic individuals to speak up for themselves.

Galatians 6:2 reminds us to "carry each other's burdens, and in this way you will fulfill the law of Christ." This scripture highlights the importance of community and mutual support. For autistic individuals, knowing that they have a network of people who will stand by them in their self-advocacy journey is empowering. Allies can offer reassurance, advice, and even advocacy on behalf of the individual when needed.

b. The Growing Autistic Advocacy Movement

The rise of self-advocacy within the autism community has given birth to a broader autistic advocacy movement. Organizations and communities led by autistic individuals are now shaping public discourse on autism, challenging outdated stereotypes, and pushing for greater inclusion in society. These advocacy movements are empowering autistic individuals to not only advocate for themselves but to also advocate for systemic changes that benefit the entire community.

Through these movements, autistic individuals are claiming ownership of their narratives, rejecting the deficit-based models that once defined autism, and instead embracing a strengths-based perspective. Advocacy groups are fighting for improved access to services, more inclusive education policies, and greater representation of autistic voices in media and leadership roles.

Isaiah 58:12 speaks of rebuilding and restoration: "Your people will rebuild the ancient ruins and will raise up the age-old foundations; you will be called Repairer of Broken Walls, Restorer of Streets with Dwellings." This scripture is a powerful metaphor for the work of the autistic advocacy movement, which seeks to restore dignity, respect, and inclusion for autistic individuals. Just as the people of Israel rebuilt their city, autistic advocates are rebuilding societal structures to be more inclusive and accepting of neurodiversity.

Conclusion: Empowerment Through Faith and Self-Advocacy

Self-advocacy is not just about asking for accommodations or speaking up—it is about empowerment. It is about autistic individuals reclaiming their narratives, embracing their unique gifts, and confidently asserting their needs in a world that may not always understand them. Through self-advocacy, autistic individuals are rising as empowered voices, showing the world that they are capable, valuable, and deserving of respect.

Faith plays a central role in this empowerment. Scripture reminds us that each individual is fearfully and wonderfully made, that God has a plan and purpose for everyone, and that we are never alone in our journey. By trusting in God's strength and guidance, autistic individuals can find the courage to advocate for themselves and live fully in the way God intended.

As we conclude this chapter, let us remember the words of Psalm 27:1: "The Lord is my light and my salvation—whom shall I fear? The Lord is the stronghold of my life—of whom shall I be afraid?" In the face of adversity, discrimination, or misunderstanding, autistic individuals can stand firm in their faith, knowing that God is with them, empowering them to raise their voices and claim their rightful place in the world. Through self-advocacy and empowerment, their voices will continue to rise.

Here are some scripture references that align with the theme "Self-Advocacy and Empowerment: Voices Rising" for Chapter 1:

1. 2 Timothy 1:7 (NIV)

"For the Spirit God gave us does not make us timid, but gives us power, love and self-discipline."
This verse speaks directly to empowerment, reminding us that God has given us a spirit of power and strength, encouraging us to use our voice boldly and with confidence.

2. Proverbs 31:8-9 (NIV)

"Speak up for those who cannot speak for themselves, for the rights of all who are destitute. Speak up and judge fairly; defend the rights of the poor and needy."
This passage encourages advocacy, urging believers to use their voices to stand up for justice, fairness, and the empowerment of those who may not be heard.

3. Isaiah 1:17 (NIV)

"Learn to do right; seek justice. Defend the oppressed. Take up the cause of the fatherless; plead the case of the widow."
This scripture calls for seeking justice and defending the oppressed, encouraging self-advocacy as a way to empower both oneself and others in challenging situations.

4. James 1:22 (NIV)

"Do not merely listen to the word, and so deceive yourselves. Do what it says."
This verse encourages action in alignment with faith, urging us to not only hear God's word but to advocate and act in ways that reflect empowerment and responsibility.

5. Philippians 4:13 (NIV)

"I can do all this through him who gives me strength."
This well-known verse is a reminder of the empowerment that comes from Christ, giving us the strength and courage to advocate for ourselves and stand strong in difficult situations.

These verses emphasize the importance of self-advocacy, empowerment, and the responsibility to use our voices in ways that reflect justice, love, and God's calling.

Chapter 12

Hidden Strengths: Uncovering Unique Talents

"For this reason, I remind you to fan into flame the gift of God, which is in you through the laying on of my hands. For the Spirit God gave us does not make us timid, but gives us power, love and self-discipline."

2 Timothy 1:6-7

Introduction: Seeing the Hidden Beauty of Autism

Autism is often framed in terms of deficits and difficulties. Individuals on the autism spectrum are frequently judged by their struggles in communication, sensory processing, or social interaction. Yet, beneath the surface of these challenges, there exists a vast spectrum of hidden strengths—abilities that, when nurtured, can shine with exceptional brilliance. While society often overlooks these talents, they are deeply woven into the identity of those with autism, reflecting the rich diversity of human experience.

In this chapter, *Hidden Strengths: Uncovering Unique Talents*, we will explore the untapped potential that resides within individuals on the autism spectrum. These talents, ranging from creativity and problem-solving to intense focus and specialized skills, are a testament to the unique wiring of the autistic mind. By recognizing and nurturing these gifts, we allow individuals with autism to not only contribute meaningfully to society but also to live fuller, more empowered lives. We will also turn to scripture to understand how

God's design includes every person's strengths and gifts, even when they are not immediately visible to the world.

As 1 Corinthians 12:4-6 reminds us, "There are different kinds of gifts, but the same Spirit distributes them. There are different kinds of service, but the same Lord. There are different kinds of working, but in all of them and in everyone it is the same God at work." This scripture affirms that every person, including those with autism, possesses unique talents bestowed by God, and these talents are part of His divine plan.

1. The Nature of Hidden Strengths in Autism

a. Hidden in Plain Sight

Individuals on the autism spectrum often possess remarkable abilities, but these strengths may not always be immediately apparent. Autistic individuals are frequently misunderstood due to differences in communication or behavior, and their talents can go unrecognized. Strengths such as hyperfocus, heightened sensory perception, or a profound ability to understand complex systems might be masked by challenges in other areas.

For example, an autistic child who struggles with traditional classroom settings might possess an exceptional memory, a strong ability to analyze patterns, or an advanced understanding of technology. However, these gifts can be overshadowed if the focus is solely on the child's social difficulties or sensory sensitivities. To uncover these hidden strengths, it requires a shift in perspective—from viewing autism through a lens of limitation to recognizing the vast potential that lies within.

In Proverbs 20:5, we are reminded, "The purposes of a person's heart are deep waters, but one who has insight draws them out."

This verse speaks to the importance of insight in uncovering hidden talents. Just as deep waters require someone to draw from their depths, autistic individuals' strengths may require someone with understanding to help bring them to the surface.

b. The Role of Neurodiversity

The concept of neurodiversity encourages us to view autism not as a disorder that needs to be "fixed," but as a different way of thinking and processing information. Autistic individuals often perceive the world in ways that are vastly different from neurotypical people, and this difference can be a source of incredible strength. Where neurotypical individuals may struggle with certain tasks, autistic individuals may excel, thanks to their unique cognitive patterns.

For example, while some autistic individuals might have difficulty with verbal communication, they may possess extraordinary visual-spatial reasoning or a deep understanding of systems and structures. These hidden strengths often provide autistic individuals with the ability to solve problems in creative and innovative ways, offering perspectives that others might not have considered.

Psalm 139:14 celebrates the individuality of each person's creation: "I praise you because I am fearfully and wonderfully made; your works are wonderful, I know that full well." This scripture highlights that every individual, including those on the autism spectrum, is wonderfully made by God with a unique design and purpose. Autism's hidden strengths are part of the beauty of neurodiversity, and recognizing them is essential for understanding the full breadth of God's creation.

2. Uncovering Hidden Strengths: Looking Beyond the Challenges

a. Observing Passion and Deep Interests

One of the hallmarks of autism is the presence of intense, focused interests. These "special interests," as they are sometimes called, are often a window into an individual's hidden talents. While these passions may seem narrow to outsiders, they frequently reveal a depth of knowledge and skill that can be transformative if nurtured.

For example, a child who becomes fascinated with trains might not simply enjoy playing with toy trains—they may develop an intricate understanding of how train systems work, memorizing schedules, learning about mechanics, or even designing their own models. What might seem like a niche interest could lead to a career in engineering, design, or logistics if properly encouraged.

Romans 12:6 tells us, "We have different gifts, according to the grace given to each of us." This scripture reminds us that every individual's passion and interest are gifts from God. By paying attention to the subjects that autistic individuals are deeply passionate about, we can begin to uncover the strengths that lie within, recognizing these interests as signposts of their God-given talents.

b. Shifting the Focus from Deficits to Strengths

A significant part of uncovering hidden strengths in individuals with autism is shifting the focus from what they cannot do to what they excel at. Too often, the world focuses on the challenges autistic individuals face—social interaction difficulties, sensory sensitivities, or communication barriers—rather than recognizing the strengths that accompany these challenges.

For instance, an autistic individual who struggles with social cues may have an extraordinary capacity for attention to detail, making them well-suited for roles that require precision, such as data analysis, accounting, or programming. Similarly, someone who finds everyday conversation difficult might be gifted in visual communication, using art, design, or technology to express ideas that transcend words.

Philippians 4:8 encourages us to focus on what is good and praiseworthy: "Finally, brothers and sisters, whatever is true, whatever is noble, whatever is right, whatever is pure, whatever is lovely, whatever is admirable—if anything is excellent or praiseworthy—think about such things." This scripture invites us to focus on the positive attributes and talents of individuals with autism. By doing so, we shift our attention from limitations to the remarkable strengths that can be nurtured and celebrated.

3. Nurturing Hidden Talents: Turning Strengths into Opportunities

a. Providing the Right Environment for Growth

Once hidden strengths have been identified, the next step is creating an environment where these talents can be nurtured and developed. For autistic individuals, this often means allowing them the space to explore their interests in depth and providing the resources needed to support their growth.

In educational settings, this might involve tailoring learning environments to the students' needs—offering flexibility in how they approach assignments, encouraging independent projects related to their interests, or providing alternative ways of demonstrating knowledge. In the workplace, it may mean creating roles that allow autistic employees to focus on their strengths, such as giving them tasks that involve detailed research, problem-solving, or innovation.

Proverbs 22:6 emphasizes the importance of guiding individuals along the path suited to their strengths: "Start children off on the way they should go, and even when they are old they will not turn from it." This verse speaks to the importance of recognizing an individual's talents early and providing them with the support needed to develop those talents. By fostering environments where autistic individuals can thrive, we help them unlock their full potential and set them on a path toward success.

b. Mentorship and Support Systems

Mentorship can play a crucial role in helping autistic individuals uncover and develop their hidden talents. Whether through formal mentorship programs or informal guidance from family members, teachers, or friends, having someone who believes in their abilities can make all the difference. Mentors can provide not only practical advice but also emotional support, helping individuals navigate challenges and stay motivated in pursuing their passions.

In the workplace, mentorship might involve pairing an autistic employee with a colleague who can offer guidance and help them adapt to the professional environment. In schools, teachers who recognize a student's potential can play a transformative role by encouraging them to pursue their interests, providing additional resources, and offering positive reinforcement.

Hebrews 10:24-25 encourages us to "consider how we may spur one another on toward love and good deeds, not giving up meeting together, as some are in the habit of doing, but encouraging one another." This scripture underscores the importance of community and support. By fostering relationships of mentorship and encouragement, we help autistic individuals build the confidence needed to fully develop their talents and pursue their God-given purpose.

4. Celebrating Hidden Strengths: Sharing Talents with the World

a. Recognizing Strengths in the Workplace

For many autistic individuals, their hidden strengths become particularly evident in the workplace when they are given the opportunity to contribute meaningfully. Employers who take a strengths-based approach—focusing on what autistic employees excel at rather than what they struggle with—can tap into a wellspring of talent that is often overlooked.

For example, autistic individuals with strong pattern recognition skills may excel in fields such as cybersecurity, data analysis, or research. Those with creative strengths might thrive in graphic design, architecture, or animation. By placing individuals in roles that align with their strengths, employers not only help them succeed but also benefit from their unique abilities and insights.

1 Peter 4:10 reminds us, "Each of you should use whatever gift you have received to serve others, as faithful stewards of God's grace in its various forms." This scripture calls us to recognize that the gifts we possess, including those of autistic individuals, are meant to be shared with the world. By creating inclusive workplaces that celebrate diversity and talent, we create environments where everyone can use their gifts to serve the common good.

b. The Power of Representation and Role Models

One of the most empowering ways to celebrate the hidden strengths of autistic individuals is through representation. When autistic individuals see others like themselves succeeding in fields such as science, art, technology, or advocacy, it reinforces the message that their talents are valuable and that they, too, can make a meaningful impact on the world.

By highlighting the successes of autistic role models—whether it's a scientist making groundbreaking discoveries, an artist creating inspiring works, or an entrepreneur starting a business—we help shift societal perceptions of autism. We move from seeing autism as a limitation to recognizing it as a source of unique strengths and contributions.

Jeremiah 29:11 offers a message of hope for those discovering and sharing their talents: "For I know the plans I have for you," declares the Lord, "plans to prosper you and not to harm you, plans to give you hope and a future." This scripture reminds us that God has a plan for every person, including those on the autism spectrum. By celebrating their hidden strengths and encouraging them to share their talents with the world, we help them step into the future that God has prepared for them.

Conclusion: Uncovering the Beauty Within

Hidden Strengths: Uncovering Unique Talents challenges us to see beyond the labels and limitations that society often places on individuals with autism. By recognizing the gifts that lie beneath the surface, we not only empower autistic individuals to realize their full potential, but we also enrich our communities and workplaces with the unique talents they bring. Through patience, encouragement, and faith, we can help uncover these hidden strengths, creating a world that values and celebrates the diversity of every person's abilities.

As we look to scripture, we are reminded that God has given each of us a purpose and a set of gifts meant to be used for His glory. In doing so, we honor the truth that every individual—neurotypical or neurodivergent—is "fearfully and wonderfully made." Let us, then, commit to uncovering and celebrating the hidden strengths of those on the autism spectrum, allowing their voices, talents, and contributions to shine brightly for all to see.

Here are some scripture references that align with the theme "Hidden Strengths: Uncovering Unique Talents"

1. 1 Peter 4:10 (NIV)

"Each of you should use whatever gift you have received to serve others, as faithful stewards of God's grace in its various forms."
This verse highlights the unique gifts and talents each person has been given, encouraging us to uncover and use them to serve others and glorify God.

2. Romans 12:6-8 (NIV)

"We have different gifts, according to the grace given to each of us. If your gift is prophesying, then prophesy in accordance with your faith; if it is serving, then serve; if it is teaching, then teach; if it is to encourage, then give encouragement; if it is giving, then give generously; if it is to lead, do it diligently; if it is to show mercy, do it cheerfully."
This passage speaks to the variety of talents and strengths each person possesses, emphasizing the importance of using them for the greater good.

3. 1 Corinthians 12:4-6 (NIV)

"There are different kinds of gifts, but the same Spirit distributes them. There are different kinds of service, but the same Lord. There are different kinds of working, but in all of them and in everyone it is the same God at work."

This verse encourages the recognition of diverse strengths and talents, all of which come from God and serve a unique purpose in His plan.

4. Matthew 25:14-30 (The Parable of the Talents)

This parable emphasizes the importance of recognizing and using the talents God has given us, illustrating that we are meant to multiply and develop our unique strengths rather than hide them.

5. Ephesians 2:10 (NIV)

"For we are God's handiwork, created in Christ Jesus to do good works, which God prepared in advance for us to do."
This verse reminds us that each person is crafted by God with a purpose, and our talents and strengths are part of His design for the good works we are called to do.

These scriptures encourage the discovery, use, and development of the unique talents and strengths God has given each of us. They highlight that every gift, no matter how hidden, is valuable in God's eyes and plays an essential role in His plan.

Chapter 13

Mental Health Matters: Addressing Co-occurring Conditions

"In the same way, the Spirit helps us in our weakness. We do not know what we ought to pray for, but the Spirit himself intercedes for us through wordless groans."

Romans 8:26

Introduction: The Overlap of Autism and Mental Health

Autism Spectrum Disorder (ASD) is a condition that influences how individuals perceive and interact with the world, affecting their communication, social skills, and behavior. While autism itself is not a mental health disorder, individuals on the spectrum frequently experience co-occurring mental health conditions that complicate their daily lives. These conditions, including anxiety, depression, attention-deficit/hyperactivity disorder (ADHD), and obsessive-compulsive disorder (OCD), often create additional challenges for those already navigating the complexities of autism.

In this chapter, *Mental Health Matters: Addressing Co-occurring Conditions*, we will explore the intersection of autism and mental health, emphasizing the need for a holistic approach to support. We will examine how these conditions manifest alongside autism, the importance of early recognition, and strategies for care. Through scripture, we'll also reflect on how faith provides strength and comfort in addressing the emotional and psychological needs of individuals with autism and co-occurring mental health challenges.

Psalm 147:3 offers solace in times of hardship: "He heals the brokenhearted and binds up their wounds." This scripture reminds us that God's healing power extends to all areas of our lives, including our emotional and mental health. By embracing faith and seeking appropriate care, individuals on the autism spectrum can find hope and healing, even in the face of significant challenges.

1. Understanding Co-occurring Mental Health Conditions in Autism

a. Prevalence and Impact of Co-occurring Conditions

Co-occurring mental health conditions are common among individuals on the autism spectrum. Research suggests that as many as 70% of individuals with autism have at least one co-occurring mental health condition, with anxiety and depression being the most prevalent. The challenges of navigating social interactions, sensory sensitivities, and communication differences can heighten stress and anxiety, contributing to the development of these conditions.

For example, social anxiety may develop as a result of repeated misunderstandings or difficulties in navigating social situations. Depression can stem from feelings of isolation, frustration, or being perceived as different from peers. Similarly, the rigidity of thought and behavior that can accompany autism may overlap with the obsessive tendencies seen in OCD. These overlapping conditions can make daily life even more overwhelming, requiring tailored approaches to care.

Matthew 11:28-30 reminds us, "Come to me, all you who are weary and burdened, and I will give you rest." For individuals with autism and co-occurring mental health challenges, this scripture serves as a reminder that God is a source of peace and rest, providing comfort in times of difficulty and uncertainty.

b. The Importance of Recognizing Co-occurring Conditions

Recognizing co-occurring mental health conditions in individuals with autism can be challenging due to overlapping symptoms. For instance, social withdrawal, which is common in both depression and autism, may be misunderstood as a natural aspect of autism rather than a sign of mental health concerns. Additionally, repetitive behaviors often associated with OCD might be mistaken for traits of autism, leading to underdiagnosis or delayed treatment of the co-occurring condition.

Early recognition is essential for ensuring that individuals receive the appropriate mental health care they need. Symptoms of anxiety, such as persistent worry, irritability, or avoidance behaviors, may be attributed solely to autism without considering the potential for an anxiety disorder. By paying attention to changes in mood, behavior, or functioning, caregivers, educators, and healthcare providers can intervene early and offer necessary support.

Psalm 34:18 encourages us with the words, "The Lord is close to the brokenhearted and saves those who are crushed in spirit." This scripture speaks to God's deep care for those who are struggling with emotional and mental health challenges. For individuals with autism and co-occurring conditions, it is important to remember that God is near, offering comfort and support in times of difficulty.

2. The Complex Relationship Between Autism and Mental Health

a. How Autism Can Influence Mental Health

The challenges of living with autism can create an environment where mental health conditions are more likely to develop. Sensory sensitivities, communication difficulties, and social misunderstandings can lead to feelings of overwhelm, anxiety, or even hopelessness. Autistic individuals may experience heightened stress in environments that do not accommodate their sensory or cognitive needs, contributing to the development of anxiety or depression.

Furthermore, the experience of feeling "different" or struggling to meet societal expectations can be emotionally taxing, leading to issues with self-esteem and identity. Autistic individuals may feel isolated or misunderstood, contributing to feelings of sadness or frustration. These emotional challenges are compounded by the external pressures of fitting into a neurotypical world that may not fully appreciate or accommodate their differences.

Isaiah 41:10 offers strength in times of adversity: "So do not fear, for I am with you; do not be dismayed, for I am your God. I will strengthen you and help you; I will uphold you with my righteous right hand." This scripture reminds individuals with autism and co-occurring mental health conditions that they are not alone—God is with them, providing strength and support as they navigate the difficulties they face.

b. Navigating the Stigma Surrounding Mental Health

Despite growing awareness of mental health issues, there is still a significant stigma attached to mental health conditions, especially when they co-occur with autism. Individuals with autism may face additional challenges in seeking mental health support due to misunderstandings about their needs or the perception that their struggles are simply "part of autism" rather than a separate issue requiring attention.

This stigma can create barriers to care, as individuals may feel ashamed or reluctant to seek help for their mental health struggles. Additionally, caregivers and professionals may not always recognize the need for mental health interventions, focusing instead on addressing the core traits of autism. Overcoming this stigma is critical for ensuring that autistic individuals receive the comprehensive care they need to address both their autism and their mental health.

Romans 12:2 encourages transformation through the renewal of the mind: "Do not conform to the pattern of this world, but be transformed by the renewing of your mind." This verse challenges us to reject societal stigma and embrace a more compassionate and understanding approach to mental health. By renewing our perspectives, we can support individuals with autism in addressing their mental health needs without judgment or shame.

3. Effective Strategies for Supporting Mental Health in Autism

a. Holistic Care: Addressing Both Autism and Mental Health

Addressing co-occurring mental health conditions in individuals with autism requires a holistic approach that considers both the individual's autism and their mental health needs. Treatment plans should be tailored to address the unique ways in which autism and mental health conditions intersect, focusing on both behavioral and emotional support.

For example, cognitive-behavioral therapy (CBT) is often effective in treating anxiety and depression, but it may need to be adapted to accommodate the communication and cognitive differences of autistic individuals. Therapy that incorporates visual aids, structured routines, or sensory-friendly environments can help make treatment more accessible and effective.

Additionally, medication may be prescribed to manage symptoms of anxiety, depression, or ADHD. However, it is important for healthcare providers to consider how medications interact with the individual's sensory sensitivities or cognitive differences. Close collaboration between mental health professionals, caregivers, and individuals with autism is essential for ensuring that treatment is both appropriate and effective.

Proverbs 11:14 reminds us of the importance of wise counsel: "For lack of guidance a nation falls, but victory is won through many advisers." This scripture emphasizes the need for collaboration and support in addressing complex challenges. By working together, healthcare providers, caregivers, and individuals with autism can create a comprehensive plan that addresses both autism and co-occurring mental health conditions.

b. The Role of Family and Community in Supporting Mental Health

Family and community support are critical components of mental health care for individuals with autism. Families can play a pivotal role by creating environments that are supportive, accepting, and accommodating to the individual's needs. This includes being proactive in recognizing the signs of mental health struggles, advocating for appropriate care, and offering emotional support.

In the broader community, schools, workplaces, and churches can also provide important support systems. Schools can offer accommodations such as sensory breaks or alternative learning environments to reduce anxiety. Workplaces can provide flexibility in hours or workspace arrangements to help autistic employees manage their mental health. Churches and spiritual communities can offer a place of belonging and acceptance, where individuals with autism feel understood and valued.

Galatians 6:2 encourages us to "carry each other's burdens, and in this way, you will fulfill the law of Christ." This verse highlights the importance of coming alongside others in their struggles. By supporting individuals with autism in their mental health journey, we demonstrate Christ's love and compassion, helping them carry their burdens and find peace.

4. Building Emotional Resilience Through Faith

a. The Power of Prayer and Spiritual Practices

For individuals with autism and co-occurring mental health conditions, faith can provide a powerful source of emotional resilience. Prayer, meditation, and scripture study can offer comfort, helping individuals manage feelings of anxiety, depression, or overwhelm. Spiritual practices that emphasize mindfulness, gratitude, and reflection can help shift focus away from negative thoughts and toward a sense of peace and purpose.

Psalm 55:22 encourages us to "Cast your cares on the Lord and he will sustain you; he will never let the righteous be shaken." This scripture reminds individuals with autism and mental health struggles that they can rely on God to carry their burdens. By placing their trust in Him, they can find strength and comfort, knowing that they are supported by His love.

b. Embracing God's Plan and Purpose

One of the most powerful aspects of faith is the understanding that each person is created with a unique purpose and design. Autism, with all of its challenges and strengths, is part of God's plan for each individual's life. By embracing this perspective, individuals with autism can find meaning in their journey, recognizing that their struggles are part of a larger story that God is writing for them.

Jeremiah 29:11 offers a message of hope: "For I know the plans I have for you," declares the Lord, "plans to prosper you and not to harm you, plans to give you hope and a future." This scripture reassures individuals with autism and co-occurring mental health conditions that their lives are filled with purpose and promise. God's plan for them is one of hope, and through faith, they can find the strength to navigate the challenges they face.

Conclusion: Faith, Support, and Healing

Addressing co-occurring mental health conditions in individuals with autism requires a comprehensive approach that considers both their mental health and their unique neurological makeup. By recognizing the signs of co-occurring conditions, seeking professional support, and creating environments that foster emotional well-being, we can help individuals with autism thrive.

At the heart of this journey is faith—faith that offers comfort in times of struggle, hope in the face of adversity, and strength for the road ahead. Through scripture, prayer, and spiritual practices, individuals with autism and mental health challenges can find resilience and healing, knowing that they are supported by God's love and by those who walk alongside them.

As we reflect on the words of Philippians 4:13, "I can do all things through Christ who strengthens me," let us remember that with faith and the right support, individuals with autism can overcome the challenges of co-occurring mental health conditions and lead lives that are filled with purpose, hope, and joy.

Here are some scripture references that align with the theme "Mental Health Matters: Addressing Co-occurring Conditions"

1. Psalm 34:17-18 (NIV)

"The righteous cry out, and the Lord hears them; he delivers them from all their troubles. The Lord is close to the brokenhearted and saves those who are crushed in spirit."
This verse emphasizes that God is near to those who are emotionally broken and struggling with mental health, providing comfort and deliverance.

2. Philippians 4:6-7 (NIV)

"Do not be anxious about anything, but in every situation, by prayer and petition, with thanksgiving, present your requests to God. And the peace of God, which transcends all understanding, will guard your hearts and your minds in Christ Jesus."
This passage encourages those dealing with anxiety or mental health struggles to turn to God in prayer, promising that His peace will guard their hearts and minds.

3. Matthew 11:28-30 (NIV)

"'Come to me, all you who are weary and burdened, and I will give you rest. Take my yoke upon you and learn from me, for I am gentle and humble in heart, and you will find rest for your souls. For my yoke is easy and my burden is light.'"

Jesus invites those struggling with the burdens of mental health and co-occurring conditions to find rest and comfort in Him, offering a lighter burden in place of their struggles.

4. Psalm 42:11 (NIV)

"Why, my soul, are you downcast? Why so disturbed within me? Put your hope in God, for I will yet praise him, my Savior and my God."
This verse acknowledges feelings of depression and despair while pointing to hope in God, encouraging those facing mental health challenges to place their trust in Him.

5. Isaiah 41:10 (NIV)

"So do not fear, for I am with you; do not be dismayed, for I am your God. I will strengthen you and help you; I will uphold you with my righteous right hand."
God promises strength and support to those who are fearful or dismayed, offering reassurance to individuals facing mental health struggles and co-occurring conditions.

These scriptures offer encouragement, comfort, and hope for those facing mental health challenges, addressing both the emotional and spiritual aspects of healing and support.

Chapter 14

Family Stories: Love, Support, and Growth

"Bear with each other and forgive one another if any of you has a grievance against someone. Forgive as the Lord forgave you. And over all these virtues put on love, which binds them all together in perfect unity."

Colossians 3:13-14

Introduction: The Power of Family in the Autism Journey

Family is a cornerstone of love, support, and growth, especially when one of its members is on the autism spectrum. Autism impacts not just the individual but the entire family unit, leading to a journey filled with challenges, moments of discovery, and opportunities for growth. Each family's story is unique, shaped by the specific needs of their loved one with autism and the strength they gain together through their experiences.

In this chapter, *Family Stories: Love, Support, and Growth*, we explore how families serve as the primary support system for individuals with autism, helping them navigate both the difficulties and opportunities that life brings. As families learn to embrace their loved one's strengths and challenges, they discover the transformative power of love, patience, and faith. We will also look at how scripture provides a framework for family members to draw strength, offering spiritual guidance that encourages families to see their journey through the lens of faith, love, and growth.

Psalm 127:3-5 reminds us that "children are a heritage from the Lord, offspring a reward from him. Like arrows in the hands of a warrior are children born in one's youth. Blessed is the man whose quiver is full of them." This passage highlights the profound gift that children represent in the eyes of God. In families that include individuals with autism, this truth takes on even deeper meaning as the challenges they face draw them closer together in love, support, and spiritual growth.

1. Discovering and Understanding Autism: The Early Days of the Journey

a. The Emotional Impact of an Autism Diagnosis

When a family first learns that their child is on the autism spectrum, it can be a time filled with mixed emotions. Some families feel a sense of relief in finally having a name for the behaviors they've observed, while others experience anxiety or grief as they come to terms with the fact that their child's development may follow a different path than expected. Regardless of the initial response, the diagnosis marks the beginning of a new journey for the entire family, a journey that will demand strength, patience, and a deep well of love.

During this phase, parents often find themselves asking, "Why us? Why our child?" The uncertainty of what lies ahead can feel overwhelming, especially as they begin to grapple with the need for specialized education, therapies, and other forms of support. Yet, this period of discovery is also one of tremendous opportunity. Families learn that autism does not define their child; it is simply a different way of experiencing and interacting with the world.

Jeremiah 29:11 offers comfort during uncertain times: "For I know the plans I have for you," declares the Lord, "plans to prosper you and not to harm you, plans to give you hope and a future." This verse reassures families that, though the path may be different, God has a plan for each individual's life, including those on the autism spectrum. By trusting in God's purpose, families can find peace and strength in the journey ahead.

b. Learning and Growing Together

As families begin to learn more about autism, they often undergo a transformation themselves. Parents, in particular, become advocates and educators, spending countless hours researching therapies, support programs, and educational options that will best meet their child's needs. They also become strong voices in their communities, advocating for greater understanding, acceptance, and inclusion of individuals on the autism spectrum.

Siblings, too, play a vital role in this journey. They learn how to interact with their autistic brother or sister in ways that foster connection and mutual respect. These relationships, though sometimes complex, can also be incredibly enriching as siblings develop deeper empathy, patience, and a sense of responsibility toward their family member.

As the family learns and grows together, they come to understand that every step of the journey brings its own unique lessons. They learn to appreciate their child's individual gifts and find joy in celebrating small victories, whether it's a breakthrough in communication, the development of a new skill, or a moment of connection that brings the family closer.

Ephesians 4:2 reminds us to "Be completely humble and gentle; be patient, bearing with one another in love." This scripture speaks to the need for patience and understanding within the family dynamic, especially when facing the challenges that come with autism. Through love and patience, families can navigate this journey with grace, growing stronger together in the process.

2. The Strength of Unconditional Love

a. The Transformative Power of Love

One of the most powerful forces in the lives of families with an autistic loved one is unconditional love. Autism may bring challenges—difficulty with communication, sensory sensitivities, or behavioral differences—but love serves as the constant, the foundation that sustains families through these struggles. Unconditional love means accepting the individual as they are, without trying to change or "fix" them, and valuing their unique perspective on the world.

For parents, this love often manifests in their tireless efforts to support their child's development. They advocate for their child in educational settings, ensuring they have access to the resources they need to thrive. They spend hours attending therapy sessions, meetings with specialists, and working on skills at home, all motivated by their deep love for their child.

Siblings, too, experience the transformative power of love. They learn to see their brother or sister's strengths, recognizing that while their sibling may communicate or interact differently, they are no less deserving of love and respect. Over time, siblings develop a bond built on acceptance, shared experiences, and a deeper understanding of what it means to love without condition.

1 Corinthians 13:7 tells us that love "always protects, always trusts, always hopes, always perseveres." This scripture perfectly

encapsulates the role of love in families with an autistic member. Through every challenge, love remains steadfast, offering hope and strength to persevere.

b. Celebrating Strengths and Individual Talents

Individuals with autism often possess remarkable talents that may go unrecognized by those who are unfamiliar with the condition. These strengths—whether they involve creativity, attention to detail, or the ability to focus intensely on a particular subject—are gifts that should be nurtured and celebrated by the family.

For example, a child who is fascinated by trains or maps may have an exceptional ability to memorize detailed information, leading to potential strengths in fields such as engineering or data analysis. A teenager who has difficulty with verbal communication may express their thoughts and feelings through art or music, offering a creative outlet for emotions that might otherwise remain hidden.

Families that take the time to discover and celebrate these strengths help build the individual's confidence and self-esteem. By focusing on what their autistic loved one *can* do, rather than on what they struggle with, families create a positive environment where everyone feels valued.

Romans 12:6 reminds us, "We have different gifts, according to the grace given to each of us." This scripture encourages families to recognize that every individual, including those on the autism spectrum, has been endowed with unique talents. By nurturing these gifts, families allow their loved one's strengths to flourish, contributing not only to the family but to the broader community.

3. Support Systems: Building a Network of Care

a. The Role of External Support

While family love and support are foundational, external support systems are also essential in helping individuals with autism reach their full potential. These support systems may include therapists, educators, medical professionals, and specialized programs designed to address the unique needs of individuals on the spectrum. For many families, the journey of finding the right support can be challenging, but it is a critical part of ensuring that their loved one thrives.

In addition to professional support, faith communities often play an important role in providing emotional and spiritual encouragement. Churches can offer a welcoming environment where families feel accepted, and individuals with autism are valued members of the congregation. Pastoral care, prayer groups, and community activities can provide additional support, helping families feel less isolated and more connected to others who share their faith.

Hebrews 10:24-25 reminds us, "And let us consider how we may spur one another on toward love and good deeds, not giving up meeting together, as some are in the habit of doing, but encouraging one another." This scripture emphasizes the importance of community and mutual support, encouraging families to seek out the networks of care that will help them navigate the complexities of autism.

b. Siblings as Advocates and Allies

Siblings of individuals with autism often take on a special role within the family. They become advocates for their autistic brother or sister, defending them in social situations and helping others understand their needs. Over time, many siblings develop a deep sense of empathy, learning to appreciate the strengths and challenges that come with autism.

In many cases, siblings also serve as allies, helping their brother or sister navigate social situations, practice new skills, or engage in activities that may feel overwhelming. This role can foster a sense of responsibility and maturity in siblings, as they learn to balance their own needs with the needs of their autistic sibling.

Galatians 6:2 encourages us to "carry each other's burdens, and in this way, you will fulfill the law of Christ." This scripture speaks to the supportive role that siblings play within the family dynamic, offering love, understanding, and practical assistance to their autistic brother or sister.

4. Growth Through Faith: Spiritual Lessons from Autism

a. Patience and Trust in God's Plan

One of the most profound lessons that families learn through their experience with autism is the importance of patience. Autism often requires families to adjust their expectations and recognize that progress may look different from what they initially envisioned. Milestones may take longer to reach, and development may follow an unpredictable path. However, through faith, families learn to trust in God's timing and plan.

Patience becomes an exercise in faith, as families place their trust in God's greater purpose. They come to understand that growth happens in God's time, and that every step—no matter how small—is part of the journey that God has laid out for their loved one.

Psalm 27:14 encourages us to "Wait for the Lord; be strong and take heart and wait for the Lord." This verse reminds families to remain steadfast in their faith, trusting that God's plan is unfolding even when progress seems slow.

b. Compassion and Empathy: Lessons for the Family and Beyond

Living with a loved one who has autism often deepens a family's capacity for compassion and empathy. As family members witness the challenges and triumphs of their autistic loved one, they learn to see the world through their eyes. This increased empathy extends beyond the family, influencing how they interact with others in their community and beyond.

Families who have walked the path of autism advocacy are often more attuned to the needs of others, especially those who may be marginalized or misunderstood. They become advocates not only for their loved one but for inclusion, kindness, and acceptance in all areas of life.

Ephesians 4:32 encourages us to "Be kind and compassionate to one another, forgiving each other, just as in Christ God forgave you." This scripture speaks to the transformative power of compassion, both within the family and in the broader community. Through their experiences, families of individuals with autism become beacons of empathy, modeling Christ's love and compassion for others.

Conclusion: Family as a Source of Love, Support, and Growth

Family is a powerful source of love, support, and growth for individuals on the autism spectrum. Through the challenges and joys of their journey, families learn the importance of patience, faith, and unconditional love. By embracing their loved one's strengths and providing the support they need, families not only help their autistic member thrive but also grow stronger together.

As families navigate the complexities of autism, they are reminded that God's love is the foundation of their journey. Through scripture, they find the strength to persevere, the wisdom to make decisions, and the faith to trust in God's plan. Together, families can create environments where love and support lead to growth—for both the individual with autism and the family as a whole.

In 1 Corinthians 16:14, we are reminded, "Do everything in love." This simple yet profound message serves as a guiding principle for families of individuals with autism. By acting in love—whether through advocacy, support, or simply being present—families create a space where growth is not only possible but inevitable. Through love, families become a source of strength, nurturing the gifts and potential of their autistic loved one while growing closer to one another and to God.

Here are some scripture references that align with the theme "Family Stories: Love, Support, and Growth"

1. 1 Corinthians 13:4-7 (NIV)

"Love is patient, love is kind. It does not envy, it does not boast, it is not proud. It does not dishonor others, it is not self-seeking, it is not easily angered, it keeps no record of wrongs. Love does not delight in evil but rejoices with the truth. It always protects, always trusts, always hopes, always perseveres."
This passage defines love and its role in family relationships, emphasizing patience, kindness, protection, and perseverance—essential elements for family support and growth.

2. Colossians 3:13-14 (NIV)

"Bear with each other and forgive one another if any of you has a grievance against someone. Forgive as the Lord forgave you. And over all these virtues put on love, which binds them all together in perfect unity."
Forgiveness and love are foundational in maintaining healthy and supportive family relationships, helping foster growth through challenges.

3. Proverbs 22:6 (NIV)

"Start children off on the way they should go, and even when they are old they will not turn from it."
This verse underscores the importance of family in nurturing growth and development, providing guidance and support from an early age.

4. Ephesians 6:1-4 (NIV)

"Children, obey your parents in the Lord, for this is right. 'Honor your father and mother'—which is the first commandment with a promise—'so that it may go well with you and that you may enjoy long life on the earth.' Fathers, do not exasperate your children; instead, bring them up in the training and instruction of the Lord."
This scripture emphasizes the mutual respect and love in family relationships, fostering growth through honoring and supporting one another.

5. Proverbs 17:17 (NIV)

"A friend loves at all times, and a brother is born for a time of adversity."
Family members, like close friends, are there to provide love and support, especially in times of hardship, highlighting the role of family in growth and resilience.

These scriptures provide a strong foundation for discussing the importance of love, support, and growth within family relationships, rooted in faith and mutual respect.

Chapter 15

Transitioning to Adulthood: Embracing Independence and Growth

"Start children off on the way they should go, and even when they are old they will not turn from it."

Proverbs 22:6

Introduction: The Path to Adulthood

The transition from adolescence to adulthood is an important and often complex period for everyone, but for individuals on the autism spectrum, this journey is particularly nuanced. Transitioning to adulthood involves not only stepping into new roles and responsibilities but also navigating the challenges of independence, self-advocacy, and personal growth. While these transitions come with unique difficulties, they are also an opportunity to embrace the strengths that individuals on the spectrum possess and to shape a fulfilling and independent adult life.

In this chapter, *Transitioning to Adulthood: Embracing Independence and Growth*, we will explore the different facets of this life stage for individuals with autism. We will address the key challenges of developing independence and navigating new responsibilities while focusing on the strengths, talents, and unique perspectives that make individuals with autism invaluable to their communities. Throughout this journey, we will look to scripture to provide guidance and encouragement, demonstrating how faith can be a powerful source of strength during times of transition and uncertainty.

Proverbs 3:5-6 reminds us to "Trust in the Lord with all your heart and lean not on your own understanding; in all your ways submit to him, and he will make your paths straight." This verse underscores the importance of trusting in God's plan as we step into new phases of life, trusting that He will guide and strengthen us as we navigate the challenges ahead.

1. The Transition to Adulthood: A Journey of Growth

a. Understanding the Unique Challenges

For individuals on the autism spectrum, the transition to adulthood can present challenges that extend beyond the typical struggles of young adulthood. Many individuals with autism experience difficulties in areas such as executive functioning, communication, and social interaction, which may affect their ability to handle new responsibilities like managing personal finances, organizing daily tasks, and navigating social and professional environments. These challenges can create anxiety, making the path to independence feel overwhelming at times.

However, with proper support and planning, these challenges can be met with confidence. The key is to approach this transition with patience and a focus on growth rather than immediate perfection. Adulthood for individuals with autism may look different from the neurotypical experience, but it is no less valid or meaningful.

Isaiah 40:31 offers encouragement during times of struggle: "But those who hope in the Lord will renew their strength. They will soar on wings like eagles; they will run and not grow weary, they will walk and not be faint." This scripture reassures us that even when the journey feels difficult, God provides the strength needed to persevere. For individuals with autism, this promise can serve as a reminder that, despite the challenges, they are never alone in their journey toward independence.

b. The Importance of Planning

The transition to adulthood for individuals with autism requires intentional planning, especially when it comes to educational and vocational pathways. As school-based services such as individualized education programs (IEPs) come to an end, individuals and their families must begin to consider postsecondary education, vocational training, or employment opportunities. This planning often begins in the teenage years and continues into early adulthood.

One of the most important aspects of planning for adulthood is setting realistic and individualized goals that reflect the person's strengths, needs, and interests. For some, this may mean pursuing higher education or vocational training; for others, it may involve finding meaningful employment or building life skills for independent living.

Proverbs 21:5 reminds us that "The plans of the diligent lead to profit as surely as haste leads to poverty." This scripture highlights the value of careful and diligent planning. By taking the time to thoughtfully prepare for the future, individuals with autism can set themselves up for success, building a foundation that supports independence and personal growth.

2. Developing Independence: Building Life Skills

a. Life Skills for Daily Living

One of the most significant aspects of transitioning to adulthood is the development of life skills necessary for independent living. These skills include everything from managing personal finances and household chores to cooking, maintaining hygiene, and navigating public transportation. While these tasks may seem simple to neurotypical individuals, they can be challenging for those on the autism spectrum, particularly if they struggle with executive functioning or sensory sensitivities.

The key to developing life skills is practice and consistency. Families and caregivers can support individuals with autism by providing clear, step-by-step instructions and using visual aids, such as checklists or calendars, to help with organization. Life skills programs and independent living training can also be valuable resources, offering structured opportunities to practice these skills in real-world environments.

For many individuals with autism, mastering life skills is not just about achieving independence—it is also a source of confidence and self-empowerment. The ability to manage one's daily life fosters a sense of accomplishment and contributes to overall well-being.

Philippians 4:13 reminds us, "I can do all things through Christ who strengthens me." This verse speaks to the empowerment that comes from relying on God's strength. As individuals with autism work to develop life skills, they can draw on their faith to find the determination and resilience needed to overcome challenges and grow in independence.

b. Social and Communication Skills

Another critical component of independence is the development of social and communication skills. For individuals with autism, navigating social interactions can be difficult, especially in new or unfamiliar settings. Understanding social cues, engaging in conversation, and building relationships are essential skills for both personal and professional success.

One way to support the development of social skills is through social skills training, which can help individuals with autism learn strategies for communication, emotional regulation, and building relationships. Additionally, opportunities for social engagement—whether through community programs, special interest groups, or church activities—can provide a safe environment for practicing these skills in real-world situations.

Ephesians 4:29 encourages us to "Let no corrupt communication proceed out of your mouth, but that which is good to the use of edifying, that it may minister grace unto the hearers." This scripture highlights the importance of communication that uplifts and builds connections. For individuals with autism, learning to communicate effectively is a key part of their growth, helping them navigate relationships with grace and confidence.

3. Navigating Education and Employment

a. Postsecondary Education and Training

For many individuals with autism, the transition to adulthood includes pursuing further education, whether through college, vocational training, or specialized programs. Postsecondary education offers opportunities for academic growth, career preparation, and the development of important life skills. However, navigating the college environment can present unique challenges, particularly when it comes to managing academic expectations, understanding social dynamics, and accessing needed accommodations.

Many colleges and universities offer disability services that provide accommodations such as extended time on exams, note-taking assistance, or quiet study spaces. It is important for students and their families to be proactive in advocating for these services and ensuring that the necessary support is in place.

Vocational training programs and community colleges can also provide valuable opportunities for skill development and career preparation. These programs often offer a more structured and hands-on approach, making them an ideal option for individuals who prefer practical learning environments.

Proverbs 18:15 reminds us, "The heart of the discerning acquires knowledge, for the ears of the wise seek it out." This scripture emphasizes the importance of seeking knowledge and pursuing education. For individuals with autism, postsecondary education and training can be a powerful tool for personal and professional growth, helping them achieve their goals and embrace their full potential.

b. Finding Employment and Career Paths

Employment is a major aspect of adulthood and independence. For individuals with autism, finding meaningful employment that aligns with their strengths and interests is crucial. While the traditional job search process may present challenges—such as navigating interviews or understanding workplace expectations, there are many pathways to success.

Vocational rehabilitation programs supported employment services, and job coaches can provide essential support in finding and maintaining employment. These services offer job training, career counseling, and assistance with the job search process, helping individuals with autism find positions that suit their skills and preferences.

It is also important for employers to recognize the value of neurodiversity in the workplace. Individuals with autism often bring unique strengths—such as attention to detail, problem-solving abilities, and creativity—that can greatly benefit their employers. With appropriate accommodations and support, individuals with autism can thrive in a wide range of careers.

Colossians 3:23 encourages us to "Work willingly at whatever you do, as though you were working for the Lord rather than for people." This scripture reminds us of the value of hard work and dedication. For individuals with autism, finding meaningful employment is not only about financial independence but also about contributing their talents and gifts to the world in a way that honors God.

4. Embracing Growth: Personal and Spiritual Development

a. Growth Through Faith

Transitioning to adulthood is not only about achieving independence—it is also about personal and spiritual growth. For individuals with autism, this period of life can be a time of profound self-discovery, as they learn more about their strengths, challenges, and identity. Faith can play an essential role in this process, providing guidance, comfort, and a sense of purpose.

Prayer, scripture study, and participation in faith communities can help individuals with autism stay grounded during times of change and uncertainty. These practices offer a space for reflection, gratitude, and connection with God, allowing individuals to draw strength from their faith as they navigate the challenges of adulthood.

Romans 12:2 encourages us to "Be transformed by the renewing of your mind." This scripture speaks to the power of spiritual growth and renewal. As individuals with autism embrace the transition to adulthood, they can find peace and empowerment in knowing that God is guiding them every step of the way.

b. Building Relationships and Community

As individuals with autism transition to adulthood, building relationships and community is essential for emotional and social well-being. Friendships, family connections, and involvement in community activities provide a sense of belonging and support. Faith communities, in particular, can offer a welcoming environment where individuals with autism feel accepted and valued.

Churches that embrace neurodiversity and foster inclusive spaces can play a vital role in supporting individuals with autism as they navigate adulthood. Whether through service opportunities, social events, or spiritual guidance, faith communities can offer a sense of belonging that contributes to both personal and spiritual growth.

Hebrews 10:24-25 reminds us, "And let us consider how we may spur one another on toward love and good deeds, not giving up meeting together, as some are in the habit of doing, but encouraging one another." This scripture emphasizes the importance of community and mutual support. By staying connected to others, individuals with autism can build relationships that uplift and encourage them on their journey.

Conclusion: Embracing Independence, Growth, and Faith

Transitioning to adulthood is a significant milestone in the lives of individuals with autism. It is a journey that requires patience, persistence, and a commitment to personal growth. While the path may be challenging at times, it is also filled with opportunities for independence, self-discovery, and spiritual development.

Through careful planning, the development of life skills, and the support of family, community, and faith, individuals with autism can embrace adulthood with confidence and hope. By trusting in God's plan and relying on His guidance, they can navigate the challenges of this transition and step into a future filled with purpose and promise.

As we reflect on the words of Jeremiah 29:11—"For I know the plans I have for you, declares the Lord, plans to prosper you and not to harm you, plans to give you hope and a future"—we are reminded that God's plan for each individual, including those on the autism spectrum, is one of growth, independence, and fulfillment. Through faith, perseverance, and the support of loved ones, individuals with autism can embrace adulthood with a sense of purpose and joy, knowing that God is with them every step of the way.

Here are additional scripture references that align with the theme "Transitioning to Adulthood: Embracing Independence and Growth"

1. Proverbs 16:9 (NIV)

"In their hearts humans plan their course, but the Lord establishes their steps."
As young adults transition into adulthood, this verse reminds us that while we can make plans, it is ultimately God who guides our steps and leads us in the right direction.

2. Isaiah 40:31 (NIV)

"But those who hope in the Lord will renew their strength. They will soar on wings like eagles; they will run and not grow weary, they will walk and not be faint."
This verse encourages those embracing independence to rely on God for strength and perseverance as they face new challenges in adulthood.

3. James 1:5 (NIV)

"If any of you lacks wisdom, you should ask God, who gives generously to all without finding fault, and it will be given to you."
God provides wisdom to those who seek it, reminding young adults that they are not alone as they grow into new roles and responsibilities.

4. 1 Corinthians 13:11 (NIV)

"When I was a child, I talked like a child, I thought like a child, I reasoned like a child. When I became a man, I put the ways of childhood behind me."
This passage speaks directly to the transition from childhood to adulthood, encouraging individuals to embrace maturity and growth.

5. Proverbs 22:6 (NIV)

"Start children off on the way they should go, and even when they are old they will not turn from it."

This verse reminds young adults that the foundations laid during their upbringing will guide them as they embrace independence and grow into adulthood.

personal growth and transformation in alignment with God's will, as they navigate the complexities of adulthood.

These scriptures offer guidance, strength, and wisdom for those transitioning to adulthood, embracing independence, and growing in their faith.

Chapter 16

Embracing Differences: Celebrating Uniqueness in Creation

"But those who hope in the Lord will renew their strength. They will soar on wings like eagles; they will run and not grow weary, they will walk and not be faint."

Isaiah 40:31

Introduction

The journey of living with and loving someone with autism often brings to light the beauty of human diversity in ways that many may never experience. While autism can present real challenges, it also offers profound opportunities to embrace differences and recognize the unique gifts that each person brings to the world. In a society that frequently celebrates conformity, those who navigate life differently—such as individuals on the autism spectrum—often invite us to broaden our perspectives and see the world with new eyes.

This chapter, *Embracing Differences: Celebrating Uniqueness in Creation*, delves into the idea that every person, regardless of their abilities or challenges, reflects the creative genius of God. By understanding that our differences are not just deviations from the norm but are part of the vast and intentional design of creation, we can learn to celebrate individuality. Living with someone who has been diagnosed with autism provides a window into the beauty of diversity, encouraging us to embrace the uniqueness that exists in each of us. In recognizing and celebrating these differences, we honor God's creative purpose and foster a deeper sense of love and acceptance in our relationships and communities.

1. The Beauty of God's Diverse Creation

a. Celebrating Variety in Nature

From the towering mountains to the smallest grains of sand, God's creation is filled with diversity. Nature itself is a testament to the beauty of variation and uniqueness. The Bible tells us in Genesis 1:31 that "God saw all that he had made, and it was very good." In this statement, we find the affirmation that every aspect of creation, in all its diversity, was intentionally crafted and declared "very good" by the Creator.

Take a moment to consider the intricate variety in the natural world. No two snowflakes are exactly alike, each leaf on a tree is slightly different from its neighbor, and even animals of the same species exhibit unique patterns, colors, and behaviors. If God created such diversity in the natural world, how much more must He delight in the uniqueness of every human being? Our differences—whether physical, cognitive, emotional, or social—are not accidents or mistakes. They are part of the grand design that makes creation rich and vibrant.

Living with a loved one who has been diagnosed with autism brings this truth into sharp focus. Autism, with its unique patterns of thought, communication, and behavior, challenges the societal preference for uniformity and invites us to celebrate individuality. It asks us to view differences not as flaws but as expressions of God's boundless creativity.

b. Made in God's Image: The Diversity of Humanity

The Bible tells us that all humans are created in the image of God (Imago Dei). Genesis 1:27 states, "So God created mankind in his own image, in the image of God he created them; male and female he created them." This powerful verse reminds us that every person, regardless of their abilities, appearance, or neurological makeup, reflects some aspect of God's nature. Autism, then, becomes a lens through which we can see the diversity of that divine image.

When we think about what it means to be made in God's image, we must acknowledge that God's image is vast and multifaceted. Just as a painting has countless strokes of color that make up the whole masterpiece, humanity is a living mosaic of different abilities, talents, and ways of perceiving the world. Autism represents one of the many shades in this mosaic—an expression of God's creativity that brings its own beauty and depth to the larger picture.

Living with someone who experiences the world through the lens of autism allows us to see aspects of the human experience that might otherwise go unnoticed. Whether it's a heightened sensitivity to detail, a remarkable memory for specific facts, or a unique way of solving problems, these traits remind us that diversity is not something to be feared or resisted but celebrated.

2. Reframing Differences: Moving Beyond Labels

a. Society's Tendency to Label

Society has a long history of labeling people based on their differences. These labels—whether they are related to race, gender, ability, or intelligence—can often serve to separate people rather than bring them together. Autism, like many other neurological differences, is frequently discussed in terms of deficits, challenges, and "abnormal" behaviors. These labels can create a narrative that focuses on what is lacking rather than what is unique and valuable.

For families and individuals affected by autism, these societal labels can be discouraging and isolating. Parents may hear terms like "low-functioning" or "developmentally delayed" and feel as though their child is being reduced to a list of what they can't do. These labels often fail to capture the full essence of the person—their gifts, strengths, and potential.

However, the Bible challenges us to see beyond these human-made labels and recognize the intrinsic worth of every individual. In 1 Samuel 16:7, the Lord tells Samuel, "The Lord does not look at the things people look at. People look at the outward appearance, but the Lord looks at the heart." This verse reminds us that God does not define us by society's labels or our outward abilities. He sees the heart, the soul, and the unique spirit within each of us.

b. A New Perspective: Seeing Through God's Eyes

When we shift our perspective from society's labels to God's vision for humanity, we begin to see the beauty in differences. Autism, rather than being a "disorder" or "problem" to be fixed, can be understood as a different way of being in the world—one that offers its own set of gifts and insights.

To see through God's eyes means to appreciate the unique way that every person reflects His image. It means recognizing that our differences are not barriers but bridges to deeper understanding and connection. Instead of focusing on what makes someone "different" in a negative sense, we can focus on how their unique qualities enrich the world and those around them.

For example, someone with autism may have an extraordinary ability to focus on a specific interest or passion for hours on end, diving deep into subjects that others may only skim the surface of. This kind of focus can be a reflection of God's own meticulous care in creation—His attention to detail and His deep understanding of all things. By embracing these differences, we celebrate the diversity of human experience and the depth of God's creation.

3. The Gifts That Come With Autism

a. Attention to Detail and Focus

One of the remarkable gifts that many individuals with autism possess is the ability to focus intently on details that others might overlook. This attention to detail can manifest in various ways, from an extraordinary memory for facts to a talent for identifying patterns in complex data. While society often values multitasking and rapid adaptation, individuals with autism remind us of the beauty and value of deep focus and dedication.

In Psalm 139:14, we read, "I praise you because I am fearfully and wonderfully made; your works are wonderful, I know that full well." This verse reflects the truth that each of us, in our unique makeup, is a masterpiece of God's design. The ability to see and appreciate detail is a reflection of the intricacy with which God Himself created the universe. Just as God knows the number of hairs on our heads (Luke 12:7) and formed every aspect of creation with care, individuals with autism often possess a gift for noticing the small, beautiful details that others might miss.

b. Honesty and Authenticity

Another gift that is often present in individuals with autism is a deep sense of honesty and authenticity. Many individuals on the autism spectrum are refreshingly direct in their communication, expressing their thoughts and feelings without pretense or hidden agendas. While this kind of directness can sometimes be misinterpreted as bluntness, it is also a profound gift in a world where people often hide their true feelings or say what they think others want to hear.

In Matthew 5:37, Jesus teaches, "Let your yes be yes, and your no be no." This instruction to speak plainly and truthfully is something that many individuals with autism embody naturally. Their commitment to honesty and authenticity can serve as a powerful reminder to all of us to live with integrity, to speak truthfully, and to be ourselves without fear of judgment.

By celebrating this gift, we honor the unique way that individuals with autism contribute to the world. Their honesty and authenticity are reflections of God's own truthfulness and faithfulness, and they remind us of the importance of living lives that are true to who we are.

4. Embracing Differences in the Family and Community

a. Fostering Acceptance and Understanding

Living with a loved one who has been diagnosed with autism requires families to embrace a different way of thinking about communication, relationships, and expectations. It challenges us to let go of preconceived notions of what a person "should" be like and to accept and celebrate them for who they are. This journey of acceptance can be transformative for both the individual with autism and their family members.

For parents, siblings, and caregivers, fostering an environment of acceptance means creating a space where differences are not just tolerated but celebrated. It means recognizing that every family member brings something valuable to the table, regardless of their abilities or challenges. This kind of acceptance can be life-changing for individuals with autism, as it allows them to feel seen, valued, and loved for who they truly are.

In Romans 15:7, we are called to "Accept one another, then, just as Christ accepted you, in order to bring praise to God." This verse reminds us that acceptance is not just a passive act—it is a reflection of God's own love and grace. When we accept one another, we reflect God's heart for humanity and bring glory to Him through our relationships.

b. Building a Culture of Inclusion

In addition to fostering acceptance within the family, it's important to extend this spirit of inclusion to the broader community. Whether it's in schools, churches, or workplaces, individuals with autism often face barriers to inclusion due to misunderstandings, lack of accommodations, or social stigmas. As a society, we have a responsibility to create spaces where everyone—regardless of their abilities—can thrive and contribute.

Creating a culture of inclusion requires both practical changes and a shift in mindset. It means advocating for policies that support individuals with autism, such as accessible education, workplace accommodations, and sensory-friendly environments. It also means challenging societal norms that prioritize conformity over diversity and recognizing that our differences are what make our communities stronger.

In Galatians 3:28, Paul writes, "There is neither Jew nor Gentile, neither slave nor free, nor is there male and female, for you are all one in Christ Jesus." This verse reminds us that in God's kingdom, there is no hierarchy of worth based on differences. We are all equal in His eyes, and we are called to build communities that reflect this truth by welcoming and including all people, regardless of their differences.

5. Celebrating Uniqueness as Part of God's Plan

a. The Importance of Every Individual's Purpose

One of the most beautiful aspects of God's creation is that every individual has a unique purpose and role to play in His grand design. Autism, like any other difference, is part of the diversity that enriches humanity and reflects the fullness of God's creation. Just as no two flowers bloom in exactly the same way, no two individuals live out their purpose in the same manner.

Ephesians 2:10 reminds us, "For we are God's handiwork, created in Christ Jesus to do good works, which God prepared in advance for us to do." This verse speaks to the idea that each of us—regardless of our abilities or challenges—has a specific purpose that God has planned for us. For individuals with autism, this purpose may look different from what society expects, but it is no less significant. Whether through acts of kindness, creative expression, or the unique ways in which they engage with the world, individuals with autism contribute to God's plan in ways that are both profound and necessary.

b. Trusting in God's Design

Ultimately, embracing the uniqueness of individuals with autism requires us to trust in God's design. It means believing that every person—regardless of their neurological makeup—was created with intention, love, and purpose. This trust allows us to move beyond the fear or uncertainty that may arise when faced with differences and instead celebrate the richness that these differences bring to our lives.

In Jeremiah 29:11, God promises, "For I know the plans I have for you, declares the Lord, plans to prosper you and not to harm you, plans to give you hope and a future." This promise extends to all of us, including those with autism. God's plan for each individual is one of hope and purpose, and by embracing the uniqueness of His creation, we participate in the fulfillment of that plan.

As we celebrate the diversity of God's creation, we honor the Creator who made each of us in His image. Autism, with its unique perspectives and gifts, is not something to be feared or fixed—it is something to be embraced and celebrated as part of the intricate and beautiful tapestry of humanity.

Conclusion: Embracing the Unseen Colors of Creation

In the journey of living with and loving someone with autism, we are invited to see the world through a different lens—one that celebrates uniqueness rather than conformity, and one that recognizes the beauty in diversity. Autism teaches us to embrace differences, to look beyond societal labels, and to see the gifts that each person brings to the world.

As we celebrate the unseen colors of creation, we come to understand that God's design is far more diverse and beautiful than we could ever imagine. Every individual, including those with autism, reflects a unique facet of God's creativity and love. By embracing this truth, we foster a deeper sense of acceptance, inclusion, and celebration in our families, communities, and the world at large. Ultimately, we are reminded that it is in our differences that we find the fullness of God's creation, and it is in celebrating those differences that we bring glory to the Creator.

Here are additional scripture references that align with the theme "Transitioning to Adulthood: Embracing Independence and Growth"

1. Proverbs 16:9 (NIV)

"In their hearts humans plan their course, but the Lord establishes their steps."
As young adults transition into adulthood, this verse reminds us that while we can make plans, it is ultimately God who guides our steps and leads us in the right direction.

2. Isaiah 40:31 (NIV)

"But those who hope in the Lord will renew their strength. They will soar on wings like eagles; they will run and not grow weary, they will walk and not be faint."
This verse encourages those embracing independence to rely on God for strength and perseverance as they face new challenges in adulthood.

3. James 1:5 (NIV)

"If any of you lacks wisdom, you should ask God, who gives generously to all without finding fault, and it will be given to you."
God provides wisdom to those who seek it, reminding young adults that they are not alone as they grow into new roles and responsibilities.

4. 1 Corinthians 13:11 (NIV)

"When I was a child, I talked like a child, I thought like a child, I reasoned like a child. When I became a man, I put the ways of childhood behind me."
This passage speaks directly to the transition from childhood to adulthood, encouraging individuals to embrace maturity and growth.

5. Proverbs 22:6 (NIV)

"Start children off on the way they should go, and even when they are old they will not turn from it."
This verse reminds young adults that the foundations laid during their upbringing will guide them as they embrace independence and grow into adulthood.

These scriptures offer guidance, strength, and wisdom for those transitioning to adulthood, embracing independence, and growing in their faith.

Chapter 17

Friendships and Intimacy: Forming Deep Connections and Growth

"Two are better than one, because they have a good return for their labor: If either of them falls down, one can help the other up. But pity anyone who falls and has no one to help them up."

Ecclesiastes 4:9-10

Introduction: The Human Need for Connection

At the core of human existence lies the need for connection—friendship, intimacy, and deep relationships that provide a sense of belonging, love, and support. For individuals on the autism spectrum, the desire for connection is no different. However, forming and maintaining friendships or romantic relationships can present unique challenges. Social interactions, communication differences, sensory sensitivities, and navigating unspoken rules of relationships require effort, adaptation, and often a deep well of patience.

This chapter, *Friendships and Intimacy: Forming Deep Connections and Growth*, explores the complexities of relationships for individuals with autism. It acknowledges the obstacles faced while also emphasizing the strengths that individuals on the spectrum possess—such as loyalty, honesty, and deep empathy. We will look at how these strengths can form the foundation of meaningful friendships and intimate relationships. Moreover, we'll turn to scripture for wisdom on how faith can help individuals with autism, and their loved ones, nurture relationships based on trust, love, and understanding.

In Proverbs 27:9, we read, "The heartfelt counsel of a friend is as sweet as perfume and incense." This passage reminds us that friendship is a blessing, a source of joy and comfort. For individuals on the autism spectrum, forming these bonds may take additional time and effort, but the rewards of deep, meaningful connections are invaluable.

1. Challenges in Building Friendships and Intimacy

a. Understanding Social Cues and Communication Differences

One of the main hurdles individuals with autism face when forming friendships and romantic relationships is the difficulty in interpreting social cues. Neurotypical interactions are often filled with unspoken signals—body language, facial expressions, and tone of voice—that can be hard for those with autism to pick up on. This can lead to misunderstandings or feelings of exclusion, both of which can make building relationships challenging.

For individuals with autism, communication tends to be more direct. They may struggle with small talk or reading between the lines, preferring clear, straightforward conversations. This can sometimes come off as blunt or disengaged to those who are unfamiliar with autism, though it is not a lack of interest or care. It's simply a different way of engaging.

Navigating these social dynamics requires patience and understanding from both sides. Those who care for or wish to form relationships with individuals on the autism spectrum must recognize the need for clearer communication, while individuals with autism benefit from understanding that relationships often involve a learning curve when it comes to social interaction.

Ephesians 4:29 offers guidance on the importance of speech in relationships: "Do not let any unwholesome talk come out of your mouths, but only what is helpful for building others up according to their needs, that it may benefit those who listen." This verse reminds us that communication—whether verbal or non-verbal—should be rooted in kindness, respect, and an intent to uplift others.

b. Sensory Sensitivities and Personal Boundaries

Many individuals on the autism spectrum experience heightened sensory sensitivities, which can complicate social and intimate relationships. Loud noises, bright lights, or crowded spaces may feel overwhelming, leading to anxiety or discomfort. Physical touch, while comforting to some, may feel invasive or unsettling to others on the spectrum, making it difficult to navigate affection and closeness in relationships.

Establishing and respecting personal boundaries is crucial for anyone, but particularly for individuals with autism. Friends and romantic partners must be sensitive to these boundaries, offering space and understanding when sensory overload occurs. Open, honest communication about comfort levels with physical affection and social environments is essential for creating relationships where both individuals feel safe and respected.

For many on the spectrum, being upfront about these boundaries allows for smoother interactions and avoids misunderstandings. Intimacy in relationships—whether emotional or physical—can only thrive when both partners feel heard and supported.

1 Corinthians 13:4-5 reminds us that "Love is patient, love is kind. It does not envy, it does not boast, it is not proud. It does not dishonor others, it is not self-seeking, it is not easily angered, it keeps no record of wrongs." This scripture serves as a powerful guide for all relationships, emphasizing that patience, kindness, and respect are foundational to building deep, lasting connections.

2. Building and Sustaining Friendships

a. The Role of Shared Interests

For many individuals with autism, friendships are often formed around shared interests or common activities. Whether it's a mutual love of science fiction, video games, art, or a specific hobby, having a shared passion can create a natural starting point for conversations and social interactions. This focus on activities can relieve some of the pressure that may come with typical social interactions and help individuals engage in ways that feel comfortable and enjoyable.

Friendships that revolve around shared interests often flourish because they provide a common ground where both individuals feel engaged and understood. It allows for focused communication and can open the door to deeper conversations as trust builds. For individuals with autism, these shared experiences can provide the foundation for lasting and meaningful friendships.

Ecclesiastes 4:9-10 speaks to the importance of companionship: "Two are better than one, because they have a good return for their labor: If either of them falls down, one can help the other up." This verse highlights the beauty of friendship—helping one another, sharing in joys, and lifting each other up when difficulties arise. Shared interests create opportunities for individuals on the spectrum to build strong, supportive bonds that embody the spirit of this scripture.

b. Developing Social Skills and Empathy

While social skills may come naturally to some, they can be challenging for individuals on the autism spectrum. However, with practice and guidance, these skills can be developed over time. Structured social skills training, role-playing scenarios, or engaging in real-world practice can help individuals improve their ability to communicate, interpret social cues, and navigate social dynamics more effectively.

Empathy, often misunderstood in the context of autism, is an important component of forming relationships. While individuals with autism may not express empathy in traditional ways, they are fully capable of deep empathy and care for others. Their empathetic responses may take the form of problem-solving or practical help, rather than emotional expressions, but they are no less sincere.

Proverbs 18:24 teaches us about the importance of strong, supportive friendships: "One who has unreliable friends soon comes to ruin, but there is a friend who sticks closer than a brother." This verse underscores the significance of loyalty and dependability in friendships. For individuals on the spectrum, developing social skills and empathy allows them to form connections that are based on trust and mutual support, building friendships that last through thick and thin.

3. Navigating Romantic Relationships and Intimacy

a. Building Trust in Romantic Relationships

Romantic relationships can present unique challenges for individuals with autism, particularly when it comes to understanding emotional expression, trust, and communication. While individuals on the spectrum are fully capable of loving deeply, they may find it difficult to express their emotions in ways that are easily understood by neurotypical partners.

Open and direct communication is key in romantic relationships, especially for those with autism. Being explicit about emotional needs, boundaries, and expectations can help reduce misunderstandings and build trust. Just as in friendships, romantic relationships thrive when both individuals are committed to mutual understanding, respect, and support.

Building trust in a romantic relationship takes time, but it can be strengthened through emotional honesty, consistent communication, and a shared commitment to the partnership.

1 Peter 4:8 reminds us, "Above all, love each other deeply, because love covers over a multitude of sins." This scripture teaches that love, when nurtured, has the power to overcome challenges and imperfections. In romantic relationships, love, combined with patience and understanding, can create a strong, trusting foundation that allows both partners to grow together.

b. Navigating Sensory Sensitivities in Romantic Intimacy

Sensory sensitivities play a significant role in romantic relationships for individuals with autism, particularly when it comes to physical intimacy. What feels comforting and nurturing to one person may be overwhelming or uncomfortable for someone with sensory sensitivities. Understanding and respecting these sensory needs is critical for fostering a healthy and supportive romantic relationship.

For some individuals with autism, physical affection, such as hugs, hand-holding, or kisses, may feel overwhelming, while for others, it may be an important form of connection. Communicating about comfort levels with touch, as well as being flexible in how affection is expressed, can help both partners feel secure and understood.

Song of Solomon 8:7 offers a beautiful image of love's resilience: "Many waters cannot quench love; rivers cannot sweep it away." This verse reminds us that true love is enduring, capable of withstanding challenges and obstacles. Sensory sensitivities, while requiring consideration and care, need not be a barrier to love and intimacy. With communication, respect, and patience, love can flourish, even in the face of sensory challenges.

4. Faith as the Foundation for Friendships and Intimacy

a. The Role of Faith in Relationships

For many individuals with autism, faith provides a solid foundation for forming and maintaining relationships. Faith communities offer a sense of belonging and provide opportunities for social engagement, spiritual growth, and emotional support. Whether through church events, small groups, or fellowship opportunities, faith-based relationships often create environments where individuals with autism can feel accepted and valued for who they are.

Faith also provides a moral and spiritual framework for building relationships. Love, kindness, forgiveness, and patience are key virtues in any relationship, and scripture offers guidance on how to apply these principles to friendships, romantic relationships, and family dynamics.

1 John 4:12 reminds us, "No one has ever seen God; but if we love one another, God lives in us and his love is made complete in us." This scripture speaks to the divine nature of love and relationships.

When we love others, we reflect God's presence in the world. For individuals on the autism spectrum, faith can be a powerful source of strength, guiding them to form relationships based on mutual love, respect, and kindness.

b. Building Relationships That Reflect God's Love

Relationships, whether platonic or romantic, are opportunities to reflect God's love in our daily lives. For individuals with autism, this means forming connections that are built on authenticity, mutual respect, and understanding. Relationships should be spaces where both individuals feel valued and accepted for who they are, without pressure to conform to societal norms or expectations.

Friendships and romantic relationships rooted in faith offer a deeper sense of purpose. They are not simply about companionship but about serving one another, growing together, and reflecting God's love in tangible ways. In these relationships, both parties learn to be patient, forgiving, and supportive, mirroring the qualities of Christ's love.

Romans 12:10 encourages us to "Be devoted to one another in love. Honor one another above yourselves." This scripture captures the essence of healthy, faith-based relationships, where love is given freely, and each person seeks to honor and uplift the other. For individuals with autism, relationships that reflect this kind of love are not only fulfilling but transformative, offering opportunities for deep connection and personal growth.

Conclusion: The Power of Love, Friendship, and Faith

Friendships and intimate relationships are essential parts of the human experience, and for individuals with autism, they are no less important. While challenges may arise in navigating social cues, communication differences, and sensory sensitivities, these obstacles can be overcome with patience, understanding, and love. Through shared interests, empathy, and clear communication, individuals on the spectrum can form deep, meaningful connections that enrich their lives and the lives of those around them.

Faith plays a crucial role in guiding relationships, providing a foundation of love, kindness, and respect. By turning to scripture for wisdom and strength, individuals with autism and their loved ones can build relationships that are rooted in God's love and reflect His presence in their lives.

As we close, let us remember the words of Colossians 3:14: "And over all these virtues put on love, which binds them all together in perfect unity." Love is the thread that binds friendships, romantic relationships, and all connections, offering a path to unity, growth, and lasting fulfillment.

Here are some scripture references that align with the theme "Friendships and Intimacy: Forming Deep Connections and Growth"

1. Proverbs 17:17 (NIV)

"A friend loves at all times, and a brother is born for a time of adversity."
This verse emphasizes the constancy of friendship and the deep bond that grows through shared experiences, especially in times of hardship.

2. Ecclesiastes 4:9-10 (NIV)

"Two are better than one, because they have a good return for their labor: If either of them falls down, one can help the other up. But pity anyone who falls and has no one to help them up."
This passage highlights the importance of friendship and support, showing how deep connections can lift one another up during difficult times.

3. Proverbs 27:9 (NIV)

"Perfume and incense bring joy to the heart, and the pleasantness of a friend springs from their heartfelt advice."
True friendships bring joy and guidance, fostering deep emotional and spiritual growth through intimate counsel and shared understanding.

4. John 15:12-13 (NIV)

"My command is this: Love each other as I have loved you. Greater love has no one than this: to lay down one's life for one's friends."
Jesus teaches about sacrificial love, the ultimate foundation for deep and meaningful connections with others.

5. Proverbs 27:17 (NIV)

"As iron sharpens iron, so one person sharpens another."
Deep friendships and relationships help people grow by challenging and encouraging each other to become better versions of themselves.

These scriptures provide a solid foundation for discussing the importance of forming and nurturing deep connections in friendships and intimate relationships. They emphasize love, humility, encouragement, and support as key elements of relational growth.

Chapter 18

Navigating Challenges: Finding Strength in Adversity

"Consider it pure joy, my brothers and sisters, whenever you face trials of many kinds, because you know that the testing of your faith produces perseverance. Let perseverance finish its work so that you may be mature and complete, not lacking anything."

James 1:2-4

Introduction

When living with a loved one diagnosed with autism, life often becomes a journey defined by a series of challenges that test emotional resilience, patience, and strength. Autism affects individuals differently, presenting varying degrees of difficulty in communication, sensory processing, behavior, and emotional regulation. For families, caregivers, and individuals living with autism, adversity can seem ever-present, whether it manifests in navigating social systems, handling day-to-day meltdowns, or simply working to understand the world from a different perspective.

Yet, in the heart of this adversity, there lies a profound opportunity to discover strength. This chapter, *Navigating Challenges: Finding Strength in Adversity*, explores the emotional, spiritual, and practical ways in which families and individuals with autism can face these difficulties with resilience and hope. It is in adversity that many find the greatest lessons in perseverance, personal growth, and faith.

1. Understanding the Nature of the Challenges

a. The Emotional Impact of Diagnosis

The first challenge many families face is coming to terms with the diagnosis of autism itself. For many parents, receiving the diagnosis is a deeply emotional experience. There are feelings of fear, confusion, and grief—fear of the unknown, confusion about what this diagnosis will mean for the future, and grief for the expectations and hopes they had for their child.

The moment of diagnosis often brings with it a range of emotions that can be overwhelming. Some parents feel relief in finally having an explanation for their child's behaviors or developmental delays, while others struggle with the sudden realization that life may not follow the path they had envisioned. These emotional responses are valid and common. Recognizing and processing these feelings is the first step toward navigating the challenges ahead.

Coming to terms with the diagnosis requires families to begin shifting their mindset from what might have been to what is—and to embrace the uniqueness of their loved one. This journey requires emotional resilience, but it is also an invitation to look at life from a new perspective and to begin celebrating the beauty and strengths inherent in their loved one's differences.

b. The Day-to-Day Realities

Autism, by its very nature, impacts nearly every aspect of life, both for the individual diagnosed and for those around them. For some, communication challenges create barriers in expressing needs, emotions, and thoughts, leading to frustration on both sides.

Others struggle with sensory sensitivities, where everyday noises, lights, or textures can trigger anxiety or meltdowns. These sensory overloads, which may seem small to those outside the autism spectrum, can feel monumental to those experiencing them.

In many cases, routines become essential. Individuals with autism often rely on structured routines to navigate their day-to-day lives, as changes or disruptions can lead to distress. For families, this can mean carefully managing schedules, creating calming environments, and avoiding situations that might lead to sensory overwhelm.

Social interactions also pose a significant challenge. Individuals with autism may struggle to understand social cues, body language, or abstract conversations, making relationships with peers, teachers, and even family members difficult at times. Parents and caregivers often find themselves advocating for their loved ones, educating others about autism, and fostering environments of acceptance and understanding.

Despite these difficulties, it is important to note that each of these challenges, while significant, can also become opportunities for growth, connection, and discovery. Each hurdle a family faces provides the chance to better understand the unique qualities of their loved one, to develop new strategies for communication, and to foster deep bonds of trust and support.

2. The Emotional and Mental Strength Required

a. Resilience Through Emotional Challenges

Resilience is the ability to adapt and recover from adversity, and for families living with autism, it becomes an essential part of daily life. Emotional challenges arise not just from managing meltdowns or difficult social interactions, but from the internal emotional landscape of parents, siblings, and caregivers. Learning to manage their own emotional reactions while supporting their loved one with autism is often one of the most demanding aspects of the journey.

Parents, in particular, may experience feelings of guilt or inadequacy. They might wonder whether they are doing enough, whether they are making the right choices for their child, or whether they could have prevented some of the challenges their family is facing. This kind of emotional pressure can lead to burnout, depression, or anxiety if not managed properly.

Building resilience starts with self-compassion. It is crucial for parents and caregivers to recognize that they are doing their best and that it is okay to ask for help, to feel overwhelmed, or to take breaks when needed. Emotional resilience does not mean being invulnerable; it means being willing to acknowledge and process emotions, to reach out for support, and to continue moving forward, even when the path is difficult.

Families can build emotional resilience through developing coping strategies, such as mindfulness practices, therapy, or simply by allowing themselves to experience and release their emotions in healthy ways. Developing these coping mechanisms can help families navigate the emotional ups and downs that are part of living with autism.

b. Mental Fortitude and Advocacy

Navigating the world as a parent or caregiver of someone with autism requires an extraordinary level of mental fortitude. From day-to-day interactions to longer-term planning, there are constant demands for advocacy and problem-solving. Parents often become experts in their child's needs and strengths, navigating complex systems such as special education, healthcare, and social services, all while ensuring that their loved one is supported.

Being an advocate means fighting for resources, accommodations, and understanding in schools, healthcare systems, and the broader community. It can mean facing down discrimination, ignorance, and resistance from others who do not fully understand the challenges of autism. This requires a level of perseverance that many may not have expected before they began this journey.

Mental fortitude is not something that happens overnight—it is built through the process of learning, adapting, and standing firm in the face of adversity. Families often find that over time, they develop a sense of empowerment through their role as advocates. This empowerment comes from knowing that their efforts are not only benefiting their loved one but also contributing to a larger societal shift toward greater acceptance and understanding of autism.

3. Spiritual Strength in Adversity

a. Finding Strength Through Faith

For many families, faith is an essential source of strength when navigating the challenges of autism. Spiritual beliefs provide a framework for understanding adversity, offering a sense of purpose and meaning in the midst of difficult circumstances. Faith also encourages hope, resilience, and the belief that there is a greater plan in place, even if the path ahead is unclear.

Turning to faith during times of adversity can bring peace and comfort. Whether through prayer, meditation, or participation in a faith community, families can find solace in the belief that they are not walking this journey alone. Scripture, for example, offers numerous passages that speak to finding strength in times of struggle. Philippians 4:13 reminds us, "I can do all this through him who gives me strength," while Isaiah 40:31 promises, "But those who hope in the Lord will renew their strength. They will soar on wings like eagles; they will run and not grow weary, they will walk and not be faint."

These verses, and many others, serve as reminders that there is a source of strength available to those who seek it. For families living with autism, leaning on faith can help provide the emotional and spiritual resilience needed to face the uncertainties and difficulties that arise.

b. Finding Meaning in the Journey

Beyond providing strength, faith also offers a way to find meaning in the journey of living with autism. While the challenges may be significant, families can draw on their spiritual beliefs to help reframe their experience in a way that brings purpose and hope. Rather than viewing autism as a barrier or a burden, families can come to see it as part of a divine plan, a unique opportunity to learn, grow, and develop new understandings of love, patience, and connection.

In 2 Corinthians 12:9, the Apostle Paul writes, "My grace is sufficient for you, for my power is made perfect in weakness." This scripture speaks to the idea that challenges, while difficult, can also be transformative. For many families, the journey of living with autism becomes a journey of self-discovery, where they learn to see beauty in the unexpected, to celebrate small victories, and to appreciate the depth and richness of life as it unfolds.

Finding meaning in adversity helps families cultivate a sense of hope and purpose. It allows them to move beyond merely surviving the challenges and into a space where they are actively finding strength, joy, and fulfillment, even in the midst of difficulty.

4. The Importance of Community and Support

a. Building a Supportive Network

One of the most critical factors in navigating the challenges of autism is the presence of a strong support network. Families who have a robust community of friends, family members, support groups, and professionals are better equipped to handle the emotional, practical, and spiritual challenges that arise. Having a network of people who understand and support the journey is essential for maintaining resilience and avoiding burnout.

Support groups, both in-person and online, can provide a lifeline for parents and caregivers. These groups offer a space where individuals can share their experiences, receive advice, and connect with others who truly understand the challenges they are facing. The sense of belonging and shared experience that comes from these groups helps alleviate the feelings of isolation that many families experience.

In addition to formal support groups, friends and extended family members play a vital role in providing emotional and practical support. Whether it's offering a listening ear, helping with childcare, or simply being there in times of need, having a supportive community can make all the difference.

b. Fostering Inclusion and Advocacy in the Wider Community

Beyond the immediate support of friends and family, advocating for broader community inclusion is essential for individuals with autism and their families. Many communities are still learning how to embrace neurodiversity, and families often find themselves in the role of educators, teaching others about autism and advocating for more inclusive environments.

This advocacy work extends to schools, workplaces, religious institutions, and social spaces. By fostering inclusion and raising awareness, families contribute to a cultural shift that values diversity and seeks to make the world more accessible for individuals with autism. This advocacy is not just about seeking accommodations but about transforming the way society views and interacts with individuals who experience the world differently.

As communities become more inclusive, individuals with autism are given greater opportunities to thrive. Whether it's through creating sensory-friendly spaces, offering specialized educational programs, or simply fostering an environment of understanding and acceptance, these efforts help ensure that individuals with autism are fully included in the life of their communities.

5. Transforming Adversity into Strength

a. Celebrating the Victories

One of the most important lessons that families learn on their autism journey is the importance of celebrating the victories—no matter how small. Every step forward, whether it's a new word spoken, a social interaction initiated, or a sensory challenge overcome, is a victory worth celebrating. These moments of progress, however incremental, are a testament to the strength and resilience of both the individual with autism and their support system.

Celebrating these victories helps shift the focus away from what is difficult and toward what is possible. It allows families to recognize the progress they have made, to honor the hard work that has been put in, and to find joy in the journey, even when it is challenging.

b. Embracing the Unique Strengths of Autism

Finally, one of the greatest sources of strength in adversity is learning to embrace the unique strengths that come with autism. While there are undeniable challenges, individuals with autism often possess incredible talents, perspectives, and insights that are not bound by neurotypical norms. Whether it's a remarkable attention to detail, a deep connection to a special interest, or an extraordinary ability to focus, these strengths offer a new way of experiencing and interacting with the world.

By celebrating these strengths, families can move beyond merely managing adversity and into a space of empowerment, where their loved one's differences are not just accepted but cherished. This shift in perspective allows families to see autism not as something to be fixed but as a unique and valuable way of being in the world.

Conclusion: Finding Strength in Adversity

Navigating the challenges of living with a loved one diagnosed with autism is a journey that requires emotional, mental, and spiritual resilience. While the path may be difficult, it is also filled with opportunities for growth, connection, and transformation. Through faith, community, and self-compassion, families can find the strength to face adversity with hope and courage.

Ultimately, it is through adversity that we discover our greatest strengths. As families embrace the unique challenges and gifts of autism, they not only navigate the difficulties but also find deeper meaning, joy, and purpose in the journey. The path may not always be easy, but it is one that offers profound opportunities for learning, growth, and the celebration of life in all its beautiful, unseen colors.

Here are some scripture references that align with the theme "Navigating Challenges: Finding Strength in Adversity"

1. Isaiah 41:10 (NIV)

"So do not fear, for I am with you; do not be dismayed, for I am your God. I will strengthen you and help you; I will uphold you with my righteous right hand."
God promises to provide strength and support during difficult times, offering hope and assurance when navigating challenges.

2. Philippians 4:13 (NIV)

"I can do all this through him who gives me strength."
This verse reminds us that we can find strength in Christ, especially when facing adversity and challenges in life.

3. James 1:2-4 (NIV)

"Consider it pure joy, my brothers and sisters, whenever you face trials of many kinds, because you know that the testing of your faith produces perseverance. Let perseverance finish its work so that you may be mature and complete, not lacking anything."
Trials and challenges are opportunities for growth, helping to develop perseverance and maturity in faith.

4. Romans 5:3-5 (NIV)

"Not only so, but we also glory in our sufferings, because we know that suffering produces perseverance; perseverance, character; and

character, hope. And hope does not put us to shame, because God's love has been poured out into our hearts through the Holy Spirit, who has been given to us."
This passage highlights the progression from suffering to hope, showing how adversity can strengthen character and faith.

5. 2 Corinthians 12:9 (NIV)

"But he said to me, 'My grace is sufficient for you, for my power is made perfect in weakness.' Therefore I will boast all the more gladly about my weaknesses, so that Christ's power may rest on me."
God's grace provides strength in weakness, and His power is revealed in our struggles, offering comfort and hope during difficult times.

These scriptures offer guidance, encouragement, and hope for finding strength during difficult times. They remind us that God is always present, providing the strength and perseverance needed to navigate life's challenges.

Chapter 19

God's Guidance: Prayer as a Lifeline

"I will instruct you and teach you in the way you should go; I will counsel you with my loving eye on you."

Psalm 32:8

Introduction

Living with and caring for a loved one diagnosed with autism is a journey filled with both beautiful moments and profound challenges. It's a path that demands patience, resilience, and a deep well of emotional and spiritual strength. In the midst of the daily demands, the uncertainty about the future, and the search for understanding, many families turn to prayer as their lifeline—a source of strength, comfort, and guidance from God. Prayer is not only a tool for seeking divine intervention but also a way to anchor oneself in faith during times of trial.

In this chapter, *God's Guidance: Prayer as a Lifeline*, we will explore the essential role of prayer for families who are navigating life with a loved one on the autism spectrum. From the emotional weight of the diagnosis to the daily challenges of caregiving, prayer offers a connection to God that provides direction, peace, and the strength to keep moving forward. Whether it's through asking for patience, wisdom, or simply the grace to make it through another day, prayer helps families tap into God's presence, reminding them that they are not alone in their journey.

1. The Role of Prayer in Times of Uncertainty

a. Finding Peace in the Storm

When a loved one is diagnosed with autism, it often triggers a whirlwind of emotions. For many families, the uncertainty of the diagnosis brings a flood of questions: *What does the future hold? How do we navigate this? Will our child find a way to communicate and connect with the world?* These questions can stir up feelings of anxiety and fear, making the path ahead feel overwhelming.

In such moments, prayer offers a refuge—a place where families can find peace amidst the storm. As Philippians 4:6-7 teaches, "Do not be anxious about anything, but in every situation, by prayer and petition, with thanksgiving, present your requests to God. And the peace of God, which transcends all understanding, will guard your hearts and your minds in Christ Jesus." This scripture serves as a reminder that prayer is not simply about asking for things but about seeking God's peace, which can calm the heart and bring clarity in moments of uncertainty.

For many families, turning to prayer in the face of an autism diagnosis helps to alleviate the emotional burden they carry. By surrendering their fears to God, they are reminded that His peace is available to them and that even in their darkest moments, He is present, offering comfort and support.

b. Trusting in God's Plan

One of the most profound challenges for families living with autism is the uncertainty surrounding the future. Autism is a spectrum disorder, which means that every individual with autism is unique in their abilities, challenges, and developmental trajectory. Parents and caregivers may wonder what the future holds—

whether their loved one will live independently, whether they will form meaningful relationships, or whether they will find a way to navigate the world in a way that makes sense to them.

In these moments of uncertainty, prayer becomes a means of entrusting the future to God. Jeremiah 29:11 reminds us, "For I know the plans I have for you… plans to prosper you and not to harm you, plans to give you hope and a future." This promise assures families that, even when the future is unclear, God has a purpose and a plan for their loved one.

Prayer is a way to release the need to control every outcome and instead trust that God's plan, though sometimes difficult to understand, is ultimately for the good of those He loves. By praying for the strength to trust in His plan, families can find the courage to move forward, even when the road ahead is unknown.

2. Strengthening Family Bonds Through Prayer

a. Uniting as a Family in Faith

Living with autism can place strain on family dynamics. The needs of individuals with autism often take center stage, and other family members may feel neglected or overwhelmed. Parents, siblings, and caregivers may experience frustration, fatigue, or even resentment as they try to balance the demands of daily life with the needs of their loved one on the spectrum.

Prayer offers families a way to come together in faith, providing a shared space where everyone can bring their burdens to God. In Matthew 18:20, Jesus reminds us, "For where two or three gather in my name, there am I with them." When families pray together, they invite God's presence into their relationships, fostering unity and mutual understanding.

Through prayer, family members can express their hopes, fears, and frustrations in a way that is both personal and collective. Parents can pray for patience and wisdom in their caregiving, siblings can pray for understanding and strength, and the individual with autism can find peace and comfort in knowing they are surrounded by a loving and prayerful family. By praying together, families create a spiritual bond that strengthens their resilience and deepens their connection with one another.

b. Finding Emotional Healing Through Prayer

Prayer also provides a pathway for emotional healing. Caring for a loved one with autism can be emotionally draining, especially when progress seems slow, or setbacks occur. Many parents and caregivers experience periods of burnout, guilt, or feelings of inadequacy. These emotions, if left unaddressed, can lead to long-term emotional strain.

In these moments, prayer offers a way to release emotional burdens. Psalm 55:22 encourages us to "Cast your cares on the Lord and he will sustain you; he will never let the righteous be shaken." By bringing their emotional struggles to God, families can find relief from the pressure to be perfect or to have all the answers. Prayer becomes a way to acknowledge feelings of exhaustion or frustration while also seeking God's grace and strength.

In addition to personal prayer, seeking out prayer from a faith community can provide additional support. Churches, prayer groups, or trusted friends can offer prayers on behalf of the family, creating a sense of solidarity and spiritual encouragement. Knowing that others are lifting them up in prayer can be a powerful reminder that they are not alone in their struggles.

3. Prayer as a Tool for Daily Guidance and Strength

a. Seeking God's Wisdom in Decision-Making

Families of individuals with autism often face complex decisions about therapies, educational options, and medical treatments. The sheer number of choices can be overwhelming, especially when there is no clear "right" answer. In these moments of decision-making, prayer becomes an essential tool for seeking God's wisdom.

James 1:5 tells us, "If any of you lacks wisdom, you should ask God, who gives generously to all without finding fault, and it will be given to you." This promise assures families that they can turn to God for guidance in making difficult choices. Whether it's deciding on the best school environment for their loved one or choosing between different therapies, prayer helps families align their decisions with God's will.

Through prayer, parents and caregivers can ask for clarity, discernment, and peace in their decision-making process. While not every decision will come with a clear answer, prayer allows families to feel confident that they are seeking God's guidance and making choices with His support.

b. Praying for Patience and Perseverance

One of the most frequent prayers for families navigating autism is the prayer for patience. Autism often involves unpredictability—meltdowns, communication barriers, and sensory sensitivities that can challenge even the most patient of caregivers. In these moments, prayer becomes a lifeline for perseverance.

Galatians 6:9 encourages us, "Let us not become weary in doing good, for at the proper time we will reap a harvest if we do not give up." This scripture speaks to the importance of perseverance, even when the road feels long and the progress is slow. Prayer provides the strength to continue loving, supporting, and caring for a loved one with autism, even on the hardest days.

By praying for patience, families can cultivate a spirit of grace and understanding, recognizing that both they and their loved one are on a journey that requires time, effort, and persistence. Prayer helps to soften the frustrations that may arise and replaces them with a sense of peace and purpose in the daily challenges of caregiving.

4. Prayer as a Source of Healing and Hope

a. Healing Through Prayer

While autism itself is not a condition that needs to be "healed" in the traditional sense, prayer can play an essential role in healing the emotional wounds that families often experience on this journey. Many families grieve the life they imagined for their loved one before the diagnosis, and others struggle with the emotional toll of ongoing challenges.

In times of emotional distress, prayer offers a path to healing. Isaiah 41:10 provides reassurance, saying, "So do not fear, for I am with you; do not be dismayed, for I am your God. I will strengthen you and help you; I will uphold you with my righteous right hand." This promise reminds families that God is with them, offering His healing and strength as they navigate their emotional pain.

Through prayer, families can ask for God's healing touch in their hearts—whether it's healing from emotional exhaustion, healing from fear about the future, or healing from the grief that accompanies unmet expectations. Prayer provides a space to release these emotions and to invite God's presence into the healing process.

b. Holding on to Hope Through Prayer

Perhaps one of the greatest gifts of prayer is its ability to cultivate hope. Autism, with all its complexities, can sometimes make the future feel uncertain or even bleak. Parents may worry about whether their child will ever achieve certain milestones, and caregivers may feel discouraged by the lack of progress in certain areas. In these moments, it is easy to lose sight of hope.

However, prayer reconnects families with the hope that God provides. Romans 15:13 offers this promise: "May the God of hope fill you with all joy and peace as you trust in him, so that you may overflow with hope by the power of the Holy Spirit." Prayer keeps hope alive, reminding families that God's plan is still unfolding, even when it's hard to see the full picture.

Prayer allows families to ask for hope in times of doubt, to seek joy in the small victories, and to trust that God's hand is at work in their loved one's life. It is through this ongoing connection to God in prayer that families find the strength to hold on to hope, even when the path ahead feels uncertain.

Conclusion: Prayer as a Lifeline

In the journey of loving and caring for someone with autism, prayer is a lifeline—a connection to God that provides guidance, strength, and comfort in the face of uncertainty. Through prayer, families can find the patience, wisdom, and resilience needed to navigate the daily challenges of autism. Prayer offers emotional healing, strengthens family bonds, and provides a source of hope that sustains them through difficult times.

As families develop a deeper relationship with God through prayer, they discover that His guidance is available in every moment of their journey. Whether it's through seeking peace in times of uncertainty, asking for strength to persevere, or finding healing in moments of emotional distress, prayer becomes a constant source of grace. It reminds families that they are not walking this path alone but are supported by a loving and present God, whose plans are always for their good.

Here are some scripture references that align with the theme "God's Guidance: Prayer as a Lifeline" for Chapter 1:

1. Philippians 4:6-7 (NIV)

"Do not be anxious about anything, but in every situation, by prayer and petition, with thanksgiving, present your requests to God. And the peace of God, which transcends all understanding, will guard your hearts and your minds in Christ Jesus."
This verse highlights the importance of turning to prayer in every situation, allowing God's peace to guide and comfort us.

2. Jeremiah 29:12-13 (NIV)

"'Then you will call on me and come and pray to me, and I will listen to you. You will seek me and find me when you seek me with all your heart.'"
God promises to hear us when we pray with sincerity and seek Him wholeheartedly, offering guidance in times of need.

3. James 5:16 (NIV)

"Therefore confess your sins to each other and pray for each other so that you may be healed. The prayer of a righteous person is powerful and effective."
This verse underscores the power of prayer, especially when offered in faith, showing that prayer can bring healing and guidance.

4. 1 Thessalonians 5:16-18 (NIV)

"Rejoice always, pray continually, give thanks in all circumstances; for this is God's will for you in Christ Jesus."
Prayer is an ongoing, vital connection to God, helping us stay in tune with His will through all circumstances of life.

5. Psalm 32:8 (NIV)

"I will instruct you and teach you in the way you should go; I will counsel you with my loving eye on you."
God promises to guide us, and prayer is a lifeline through which we receive His counsel and direction.

These scriptures emphasize the power of prayer as a lifeline for guidance, strength, and connection with God in all circumstances. They remind us that through prayer, we can trust in God's constant presence and direction.

Chapter 20

The Power of Perspective: Viewing Life Through a Different Lens

"'For my thoughts are not your thoughts, neither are your ways my ways,' declares the Lord. 'As the heavens are higher than the earth, so are my ways higher than your ways and my thoughts than your thoughts."

Isaiah 55:8-9

Introduction

Living with a loved one diagnosed with autism is a journey that continually shifts the lens through which we see the world. Autism challenges many of the traditional views of what it means to communicate, connect, and experience life. At times, it demands that we redefine our expectations, adjust our perceptions, and learn to embrace a new kind of normal. For families and caregivers, this process is transformative, often requiring a complete change in how life is viewed and experienced.

This chapter, *The Power of Perspective: Viewing Life Through a Different Lens*, explores the impact of perspective in the context of living with autism. By reframing how we see the challenges and triumphs of our loved ones, we discover a deeper appreciation for their uniqueness and the beauty of their differences. Perspective shifts allow us to see beyond the daily struggles and into the richness of life's details that might otherwise go unnoticed. It is through these new ways of seeing that we can grow in patience, understanding, and love—finding joy in the unexpected and strength in adversity.

1. Shifting from Expectations to Acceptance

a. Confronting Initial Expectations

Before a child is born, parents often have dreams and expectations for their future. These ideas are usually based on societal norms—hitting milestones such as first words, first steps, academic success, friendships, and eventually independence. When a child is diagnosed with autism, those expectations can suddenly feel uncertain or even unattainable, leading parents and families to grapple with feelings of loss, grief, and confusion.

The weight of unmet expectations can feel overwhelming, as families begin to realize that the future they had imagined may not unfold as planned. This emotional response is natural, and it is important to recognize and validate these feelings. Autism, with its wide spectrum of behaviors and developmental paths, often requires parents to let go of traditional timelines and expectations, and instead embrace a future that is uniquely tailored to their child's needs and strengths.

b. Moving Toward Acceptance

Acceptance is not about lowering expectations or giving up on dreams for a loved one with autism; rather, it's about adjusting to a new reality and discovering the beauty within it. When families shift their perspective from focusing on what their child "should" be doing to celebrating who their child *is*, they open the door to a deeper level of understanding and joy. This shift allows parents and caregivers to recognize the incredible progress their loved one makes, even if it doesn't align with conventional milestones.

Acceptance also means seeing the world through their loved one's eyes and understanding that different doesn't mean deficient. Autism brings with it a new way of experiencing life, and by embracing that, families can learn to celebrate their loved one's strengths and abilities, rather than focusing on what society might perceive as limitations.

As 1 Samuel 16:7 reminds us, "The Lord does not look at the things people look at. People look at the outward appearance, but the Lord looks at the heart." This perspective encourages families to see their loved ones not through the lens of societal expectations but through the lens of love and acceptance—seeing the heart and soul of the person who experiences life differently.

2. Embracing the Gift of a New Perspective

a. A Different View of Time and Progress

In a world that values rapid progress, quick achievements, and constant forward momentum, autism often challenges the conventional view of development. Many individuals on the autism spectrum develop at their own pace, following a timeline that doesn't always align with societal expectations. This can be frustrating for families, particularly when it feels like progress is slow or inconsistent. However, autism also offers a profound gift—the opportunity to redefine what progress looks like and to appreciate the small, meaningful victories along the way.

Families living with autism are often reminded that success doesn't have to be measured by how quickly or easily someone reaches a goal. Instead, success can be found in the small moments of growth, whether it's a new word spoken, a behavior mastered, or a social connection made. These moments, while they may seem small to outsiders, are monumental for families and individuals with autism. They represent not just progress but perseverance, patience, and resilience.

This shift in perspective teaches families to slow down and to value progress in a different way. It allows them to see the beauty in the journey, rather than focusing solely on the destination. Patience becomes not just a virtue but a way of life, as families learn to trust that their loved one is progressing exactly as they are meant to, in their own time and in their own way.

Romans 12:12 encourages us to "be joyful in hope, patient in affliction, faithful in prayer." Patience, in this context, is not passive; it is an active engagement in the process of growth, trusting that God's timing is perfect even when it doesn't align with our expectations.

b. Sensory Awareness: Seeing the World Through a New Lens

Many individuals with autism experience heightened sensory awareness, meaning they are more sensitive to sounds, lights, textures, and even emotions. While this sensitivity can sometimes lead to sensory overload, it also offers a unique way of experiencing the world. What might go unnoticed by most people—such as the pattern of light streaming through a window or the subtle sound of leaves rustling in the wind—can become moments of intense focus and joy for someone with autism.

As caregivers and family members, learning to view the world through this sensory lens can be transformative. It invites us to slow down and appreciate the beauty in the details that we might otherwise overlook. A child's fascination with the texture of a fabric or the rhythm of a song reminds us that there is beauty in simplicity and that the world is full of small wonders waiting to be noticed.

This heightened sensory experience can also be a source of joy and connection for families. By engaging with their loved one's sensory world—whether it's through music, nature, or favorite activities—families can form deep bonds and share in the delight that comes from experiencing life in vivid detail.

Autism invites us to see the world not as a place to be rushed through but as a space to be savored. It teaches us that there is value in observing, in listening, and in truly being present with the world around us.

3. Cultivating Resilience Through a Shift in Perspective

a. Reframing Challenges as Opportunities

Living with autism presents numerous challenges—whether it's navigating social interactions, managing sensory sensitivities, or dealing with communication difficulties. These challenges can be overwhelming at times, leading families to feel frustrated, exhausted, or even defeated. However, by shifting perspective, families can begin to see these challenges not as insurmountable obstacles but as opportunities for growth, both for their loved one with autism and for themselves.

Every challenge faced is an opportunity to develop new skills, discover new ways of communicating, or find creative solutions to problems. For example, a child who struggles with verbal communication may develop an incredible ability to express themselves through art, music, or technology. A teenager who finds social interactions difficult may build deep, meaningful relationships with a small group of trusted friends. By reframing challenges as opportunities, families can begin to see the strengths and potential that exist within their loved one.

This shift in perspective also fosters resilience. It reminds families that while the journey may be difficult, they have the strength and capacity to adapt and grow. Each obstacle overcome is a testament to the resilience of both the individual with autism and their family, reinforcing the belief that they are capable of facing whatever challenges come their way.

In James 1:2-4, we are reminded, "Consider it pure joy, my brothers and sisters, whenever you face trials of many kinds, because you know that the testing of your faith produces perseverance." This scripture encourages us to view trials not as setbacks but as opportunities for growth and transformation, and it is through these trials that we develop the perseverance needed to navigate life's difficulties with grace and strength.

b. Strength in Diversity

Autism challenges the conventional ideas of what it means to be "normal," inviting us to embrace neurodiversity as a strength rather than a limitation. Each person with autism brings their own unique set of strengths, talents, and perspectives to the world. Whether it's an incredible memory, a deep passion for a specific subject, or an ability to think creatively outside the box, individuals with autism contribute to the richness and diversity of human experience.

By shifting our perspective to focus on the strengths of autism, we begin to see how neurodiversity enriches our world. Instead of viewing autism as something to be fixed or cured, we can celebrate the ways in which it brings new ideas, fresh perspectives, and creative solutions to problems. This shift in perspective allows us to move away from a deficit-based view of autism and toward one that recognizes and honors the gifts that individuals with autism bring to our lives.

As caregivers and family members, it is essential to support and nurture these strengths, providing opportunities for our loved ones to explore their interests and develop their talents. Whether it's through specialized programs, hobbies, or creative outlets, families can help their loved ones with autism thrive in areas where they excel, fostering a sense of confidence and self-worth.

4. Faith as a Foundation for Perspective

a. Trusting in God's Plan

For many families, faith is the foundation upon which their perspective is built. Faith provides a framework for understanding the challenges of autism, offering hope, comfort, and a sense of purpose in the midst of difficulty. When families place their trust in God, they are reminded that, although the path may be challenging, there is a greater plan at work—a plan that is full of grace, love, and divine purpose.

In Proverbs 3:5-6, we are encouraged to "Trust in the Lord with all your heart and lean not on your own understanding; in all your ways submit to him, and he will make your paths straight." This scripture speaks to the importance of surrendering our need for control and trusting that God's plan is greater than our own. For families navigating life with autism, this trust in God's plan can provide peace and reassurance, even when the future feels uncertain.

Faith helps to anchor families in a perspective that is rooted in hope. It reminds them that they are not walking this journey alone—that God is with them every step of the way, providing guidance, strength, and comfort in times of need.

b. The Role of Prayer in Shifting Perspective

Prayer is a powerful tool for shifting perspective, offering families the opportunity to seek God's guidance and wisdom in moments of difficulty. Through prayer, families can ask for the strength to see their loved one's challenges through God's eyes, to find joy in the small victories, and to remain hopeful even in the face of adversity.

Prayer helps to reframe the way families view their circumstances. It provides a space for reflection, where they can release their fears, frustrations, and anxieties to God, trusting that He is working in ways they may not yet see. Prayer is not just a request for help; it is a means of connecting with God's love and grace, allowing families to gain a new perspective on the challenges they face.

Colossians 4:2 encourages us to "Devote yourselves to prayer, being watchful and thankful." By committing to prayer, families open themselves to God's presence and His ability to transform their perspective. It is through this ongoing connection with God that families find the strength to continue their journey with hope, faith, and renewed purpose.

5. The Transformative Power of Perspective

a. Seeing the Beauty in the Struggle

One of the most transformative aspects of perspective is the ability to see beauty in the midst of struggle. Autism, while challenging, also offers moments of profound beauty—whether it's the joy of a child's laughter, the breakthrough in communication, or the simple act of connection. These moments, while they may seem small, carry immense significance for families, reminding them that beauty can be found even in the most difficult circumstances.

By shifting their perspective to focus on these moments of beauty, families can experience a deeper sense of gratitude and appreciation for their loved one with autism. They learn to celebrate the small victories and to find joy in the unexpected. This perspective shift helps to alleviate the weight of daily challenges, replacing it with a sense of wonder and appreciation for the uniqueness of their loved one's journey.

b. The Gift of Growth

Perspective also allows families to recognize the personal growth that comes from living with autism. While the journey may be difficult, it is also one of profound transformation. Families grow in patience, compassion, empathy, and resilience as they navigate the complexities of autism. They learn to see the world through a different lens—one that is full of grace, love, and understanding.

This growth extends beyond the individual with autism and touches every member of the family. Siblings, parents, and caregivers all experience their own transformation as they learn to adapt, to support one another, and to find strength in their shared journey. Autism, in this way, becomes not just a challenge but a catalyst for personal and spiritual growth, shaping families in ways that are both unexpected and deeply meaningful.

Conclusion: The Power of Perspective

The journey of living with a loved one diagnosed with autism requires a continual shift in perspective. It calls families to see the world through a different lens—one that values progress over perfection, resilience over ease, and love over expectations. By embracing this new perspective, families discover a deeper appreciation for the uniqueness of their loved one's journey, finding joy in the small victories and strength in the face of adversity.

Through faith, patience, and a commitment to seeing the beauty in every moment, families are able to navigate the challenges of autism with grace and hope. This shift in perspective transforms not only how they view autism but how they experience life itself—opening their hearts to the richness and depth of life's unseen colors.

Here are some scripture references that align with the theme "The Power of Perspective: Viewing Life Through a Different Lens" for Chapter 1:

1. Romans 12:2 (NIV)

"Do not conform to the pattern of this world, but be transformed by the renewing of your mind. Then you will be able to test and approve what God's will is—his good, pleasing and perfect will."
This verse encourages a transformation of the mind, helping us to view life through a new, godly perspective rather than through worldly standards.

2. 2 Corinthians 5:7 (NIV)

"For we live by faith, not by sight."
This verse reminds us to trust in God's plan and view life through the lens of faith, rather than solely through what we see and experience in the physical world.

3. Proverbs 3:5-6 (NIV)

"Trust in the Lord with all your heart and lean not on your own understanding; in all your ways submit to him, and he will make your paths straight."
This passage calls for trusting God's perspective over our own, helping us shift our view from our limited understanding to His broader, wiser one.

4. Isaiah 55:8-9 (NIV)

"'For my thoughts are not your thoughts, neither are your ways my ways,' declares the Lord. 'As the heavens are higher than the earth, so are my ways higher than your ways and my thoughts than your thoughts.'"
God's perspective is infinitely greater than ours, and this scripture helps us remember to trust His view of our lives, even when we don't fully understand it.

5. Colossians 3:2 (NIV)

"Set your minds on things above, not on earthly things."
This verse encourages us to focus on heavenly, eternal matters, shifting our perspective away from earthly concerns and temporary challenges.

These scriptures emphasize the transformative power of viewing life from God's perspective, shifting our focus from earthly limitations to eternal possibilities, and encouraging faith and hope in the unseen.

Chapter 21

Understanding Autism: A Spectrum, not a Label

"For we are God's handiwork, created in Christ Jesus to do good works, which God prepared in advance for us to do."

Ephesians 2:10

Introduction

Autism is often misunderstood, reduced to a single, rigid definition that doesn't capture the incredible diversity of experiences within the spectrum. This misunderstanding has led to stereotypes and assumptions that don't reflect the reality of those living with autism or their loved ones. To understand autism as a spectrum rather than a label is to acknowledge its multifaceted nature—its challenges, its strengths, and the individuality of each person it touches.

Autism Spectrum Disorder (ASD) is just that: a spectrum. It encompasses a wide range of behaviors, abilities, and challenges, each as unique as the individual living with them. No two people with autism are alike. For families living with a loved one who has been diagnosed with autism, this spectrum manifests in both expected and unexpected ways. It can be both isolating and enriching, frustrating and enlightening. Understanding autism as a spectrum allows us to see beyond the limitations of a label, embracing the richness of diversity that comes with it.

In this chapter, we'll explore the nuanced nature of autism, breaking down common misconceptions, highlighting the strengths of those on the spectrum, and offering insight into the day-to-day realities of life with a loved one diagnosed with autism. By moving beyond the label, we can open the door to a deeper, more compassionate understanding of what it means to live with autism—and what it means to love someone who does.

Autism: Beyond the Stereotypes

When most people think of autism, a narrow set of characteristics comes to mind—difficulty with social interaction, repetitive behaviors, or an aversion to change. These traits are commonly associated with autism, but they don't represent the full picture. The idea that autism can be summed up by a checklist of symptoms oversimplifies a deeply complex and varied condition.

One of the most common misconceptions is that all individuals with autism are the same, with similar behaviors, challenges, and abilities. This is far from true. Autism manifests differently in every person. Some individuals may be non-verbal and rely on alternative forms of communication, while others may have highly developed language skills but struggle with the subtleties of social interaction. Some people on the spectrum are sensitive to sensory stimuli like bright lights or loud noises, while others might seek out those very same stimuli.

There is no "one-size-fits-all" description of autism. It is a spectrum, and individuals can fall anywhere along that spectrum. The term "spectrum" reflects this range, emphasizing that while all individuals with autism share certain core characteristics, the ways in which those characteristics manifest can be vastly different.

This is why it's critical to resist the urge to define individuals with autism solely based on their diagnosis. Too often, the label of autism is seen as a limiting factor, focusing on what a person *can't* do rather than what they *can*. But if we take the time to look beyond the label, we begin to see the unique strengths and talents that individuals with autism possess, along with the many ways they contribute to the world.

The Spectrum of Abilities

One of the most beautiful aspects of autism is the incredible diversity of abilities that exists within the spectrum. While some individuals may struggle in one area, they often excel in another. This diversity is a reminder that every individual on the spectrum is capable of growth, development, and contribution—each in their own way.

Many people with autism have heightened abilities in specific areas, such as mathematics, music, art, or memory. These strengths often defy conventional expectations. For example, some individuals on the spectrum may have an extraordinary ability to recall specific details from years past or solve complex puzzles with ease. Others may possess a deep understanding of a particular topic, allowing them to become experts in their field of interest.

Yet, these talents can sometimes go unrecognized, overshadowed by the challenges that autism can present. It's easy to focus on what is perceived as a deficit, such as difficulty with social cues or sensitivity to sensory stimuli, but doing so limits our understanding of the individual as a whole. The truth is, many individuals with autism have an extraordinary capacity for focus and attention to detail—skills that, when nurtured, can lead to significant achievements.

However, the flip side of this coin is that individuals with autism often struggle in areas where others may not. For some, daily tasks like getting dressed, navigating social settings, or maintaining eye contact can be overwhelming. These challenges, while real and impactful, do not diminish the strengths and talents that coexist alongside them.

Understanding autism as a spectrum requires us to hold space for both the challenges and the strengths that individuals with autism experience. It means recognizing that every person on the spectrum has a unique combination of abilities, and that no two journeys with autism are the same.

The Impact of Sensory Processing Differences

One of the core challenges faced by individuals with autism is sensory processing differences. For many, the world is a barrage of overwhelming stimuli—bright lights, loud sounds, strong smells, and even textures can be difficult to navigate. These sensory experiences, which may seem benign to neurotypical individuals, can cause significant distress for someone on the autism spectrum.

Sensory sensitivities are a common characteristic of autism, and they can affect everything from how a person interacts with their environment to how they communicate. Some individuals may become easily overstimulated in noisy environments, while others may seek out sensory input to regulate their emotions or calm themselves. This can manifest in repetitive behaviors like rocking, flapping, or humming, which serve as self-soothing mechanisms in response to sensory overload.

For families living with a loved one who has sensory sensitivities, everyday tasks can present unique challenges. A simple trip to the grocery store, for instance, can turn into a difficult experience if the fluorescent lights are too bright or the crowds too loud. Understanding the impact of sensory processing differences is essential for creating an environment where individuals with autism can thrive.

However, it's important to note that not all sensory experiences are negative for those on the spectrum. Some individuals have a heightened appreciation for sensory input that others might overlook. They might be drawn to specific textures, colors, or sounds, finding beauty and comfort in these sensory experiences. For example, the feel of a particular fabric or the sound of a certain instrument might bring immense joy to someone on the spectrum, offering a sense of calm and security.

Sensory processing differences are a reminder that the world is experienced in profoundly diverse ways by individuals with autism. By understanding and accommodating these differences, we can help create a more inclusive and supportive environment for those on the spectrum.

Social Interaction: A Different Approach

Social interaction can be one of the most challenging aspects of life for individuals with autism, and it's an area where the spectrum truly shines in its diversity. While some people on the spectrum may struggle with traditional social norms—such as maintaining eye contact, interpreting body language, or engaging in small talk—others may be highly social but in ways that are different from neurotypical expectations.

One of the common misconceptions about autism is that individuals on the spectrum are uninterested in social interaction or lack the capacity for empathy. In reality, many people with autism are deeply empathetic and care about forming relationships, but they may express these desires differently. For instance, someone with autism might prefer engaging in deep, meaningful conversations about a topic of interest rather than participating in casual social exchanges. They may also show affection or care through actions rather than words, or through interests and activities that are meaningful to them.

It's important to recognize that the social challenges faced by individuals with autism are not due to a lack of interest in connecting with others but rather differences in how they process social information. For some, social cues like facial expressions, tone of voice, or implied meanings may be difficult to interpret. This can lead to misunderstandings, where neurotypical individuals perceive someone with autism as being aloof or disinterested, when in reality, they are simply processing social interactions differently.

Building social connections for individuals on the spectrum often requires a supportive environment where their unique communication styles are respected and understood. For families, this might mean finding social activities that align with their loved one's interests or working with professionals who can help develop social skills in a way that is meaningful to the individual. It also means encouraging neurotypical peers and friends to approach social interactions with curiosity and openness, rather than judgment.

By fostering an environment of acceptance and understanding, we can help individuals with autism develop meaningful social connections on their own terms.

The Role of Routine and Structure

For many individuals with autism, routine and structure provide a sense of security and predictability in an otherwise chaotic world.

Changes in routine—no matter how small—can be distressing and lead to feelings of anxiety or discomfort. This reliance on routine is not about inflexibility but rather a need for consistency in an environment that often feels overwhelming.

For families living with a loved one diagnosed with autism, establishing routines can be a key part of creating a supportive home environment. Predictability in daily schedules, meal times, or bedtime routines can help alleviate some of the anxiety that comes with change. However, it's also important to balance routine with flexibility, gradually introducing new experiences or changes in a way that feels manageable for the individual.

While routine is essential for many individuals on the spectrum, it's important to recognize that this does not mean they are incapable of handling change or new experiences. In fact, with the right support, individuals with autism can learn to adapt to new situations and even thrive in them. The key is providing a supportive framework that acknowledges their need for structure while also gently encouraging growth and flexibility.

For example, preparing a child with autism for an upcoming change—such as a new school year or a family vacation—can involve using visual schedules, social stories, or role-playing to help them understand what to expect. By giving individuals with autism the tools to navigate new experiences, we can help reduce anxiety and build confidence in their ability to handle change.

The Power of Special Interests

One of the most fascinating aspects of autism is the presence of special interests—deep, focused areas of interest that individuals on the spectrum often pursue with passion and intensity. These interests can vary widely, from trains and dinosaurs to complex mathematical theories or intricate art forms. For many individuals with autism, special interests are not just hobbies; they are sources of joy, comfort, and a sense of purpose.

Special interests offer a window into the unique ways in which individuals with autism experience the world. These interests often provide a sense of mastery and control, offering a refuge from the sensory and social challenges that can be overwhelming. In many cases, individuals with autism develop an extraordinary depth of knowledge in their area of interest, allowing them to become experts in their chosen field.

For families living with a loved one who has autism, embracing these special interests is an important part of supporting their emotional and intellectual growth. While it can be easy to dismiss a child's fascination with a particular topic as obsessive or narrow, it's important to recognize the value that these interests hold for the individual. Special interests can be used as a tool for learning, communication, and social engagement, providing a bridge to deeper connections with others.

For example, a child with autism who is passionate about animals might use their knowledge of different species to engage with peers or participate in activities like visiting the zoo or volunteering at an animal shelter. These interests can also be leveraged in educational settings, allowing children to use their strengths to excel in subjects that might otherwise be challenging.

By encouraging and nurturing special interests, we can help individuals with autism build confidence, develop new skills, and find joy in the world around them.

Advocacy and Acceptance

Understanding autism as a spectrum, not a label, is crucial not only for individuals with autism but for the broader society in which they live. Advocacy and acceptance are key components of this understanding. Too often, individuals with autism are marginalized or misunderstood, facing barriers in education, employment, and social settings. This is not due to any inherent deficit in the individuals themselves but rather a lack of understanding and acceptance on the part of society.

Advocating for individuals with autism means challenging the stereotypes and misconceptions that surround the condition. It means creating inclusive environments where people on the spectrum are valued for their strengths, not defined by their challenges. It means pushing for better access to resources, support services, and opportunities for individuals with autism to thrive in their communities.

For families, advocacy begins at home. It involves educating others about autism, raising awareness about the spectrum of abilities and challenges that exist, and fighting for the rights of their loved ones to receive the support they need. It also means modeling acceptance and understanding, both within the family unit and in the wider community.

Acceptance, however, goes beyond mere tolerance. It involves embracing the unique ways in which individuals with autism experience and interact with the world. It means recognizing that there is no one "right" way to communicate, learn, or engage with others. By accepting and celebrating the diversity of the autism spectrum, we create a more inclusive society where everyone can thrive.

Conclusion: Moving Beyond the Label

Autism is not a label; it is a spectrum—a wide, diverse range of experiences, abilities, and challenges. By understanding autism as a spectrum, we move beyond the limitations of a diagnosis and begin to see the full, rich humanity of those living with it. Every person with autism has a unique story, filled with strengths, challenges, joys, and struggles. These stories deserve to be heard and understood, not through the narrow lens of a label but through the broader understanding of what it means to live, love, and thrive on the spectrum.

As we continue to learn about autism, it's essential to remember that the spectrum is not a limitation but a reflection of the incredible diversity of human experience. By embracing this diversity, we can create a world where individuals with autism are not just accepted but celebrated for the unique gifts they bring into our lives.

Here are some scripture references that align with the theme "Understanding Autism: A Spectrum, Not a Label" for Chapter 1:

1. Psalm 139:13-14 (NIV)

"For you created my inmost being you knit me together in my mother's womb. I praise you because I am fearfully and wonderfully made; your works are wonderful; I know that full well."
This verse reminds us that every person, regardless of abilities or challenges, is uniquely created by God and is wonderfully made. It encourages us to see individuals beyond labels, recognizing their inherent value.

2. 1 Corinthians 12:18-20 (NIV)

"But in fact God has placed the parts in the body, every one of them, just as he wanted them to be. If they were all one part, where would the body be? As it is, there are many parts, but one body."
This passage highlights the diversity of God's creation, emphasizing that every person has a unique role and purpose. It's a reminder that individuals with autism are valuable parts of the body of Christ, contributing in their own distinct ways.

3. 1 Samuel 16:7 (NIV)

"But the Lord said to Samuel, 'Do not consider his appearance or his height, for I have rejected him. The Lord does not look at the things people look at. People look at the outward appearance, but the Lord looks at the heart.'"
This verse encourages us to see beyond outward appearances or labels and focus on the heart and soul of each person, as God does.

4. Romans 12:4-6 (NIV)

"For just as each of us has one body with many members, and these members do not all have the same function, so in Christ we, though many, form one body, and each member belongs to all the others. We have different gifts, according to the grace given to each of us."
This passage emphasizes that everyone has unique gifts and roles. Autism, as part of the spectrum of human diversity, brings unique strengths and perspectives to the community.

5. Ephesians 2:10 (NIV)

"For we are God's handiwork, created in Christ Jesus to do good works, which God prepared in advance for us to do."

This verse speaks to the idea that every person is intentionally created by God with a purpose, encouraging us to see individuals with autism as part of God's masterpiece, each with their own role in His plan.

These scriptures offer guidance on understanding autism as part of the diversity of God's creation and remind us to embrace and value each individual as fearfully and wonderfully made. They encourage love, acceptance, and appreciation for the unique gifts and perspectives that everyone brings, regardless of labels.

Chapter 22

The History of Autism: From Misunderstanding to Awareness

"If any of you lacks wisdom, you should ask God, who gives generously to all without finding fault, and it will be given to you."

James 1:5

Autism is a word that many people today are familiar with, but for centuries, individuals on the spectrum were misunderstood and mislabeled. The journey from misunderstanding to awareness has been long and filled with societal and scientific progress, as well as many personal battles fought by individuals and families. Autism Spectrum Disorder (ASD) is now understood to encompass a wide variety of symptoms and traits, ranging from difficulties with social interactions to unique talents in specific areas. Yet, this understanding has only been achieved after decades of evolving knowledge, from the earliest clinical descriptions to modern-day advocacy for acceptance and inclusion.

In this chapter, we'll explore the history of autism, a story of progress but also one of setbacks, misdiagnoses, and profound challenges. For families living with a loved one who has been diagnosed with autism, this historical context is crucial in understanding the road to awareness and acceptance. By looking at where we have come from, we can better appreciate how far we still need to go—not only in scientific understanding but in societal inclusion and support.

Early Misunderstandings: A Misdiagnosed Condition

For much of history, individuals with autism were misunderstood and mislabeled. In ancient times and well into the 19th century, people who exhibited behaviors we now associate with autism—difficulty with social interactions, limited speech, or repetitive movements—were often seen as being mentally ill, intellectually disabled, or even possessed. Without the knowledge of neurological diversity, many individuals were institutionalized or hidden away by families ashamed of their differences. Sadly, the earliest forms of understanding were more about exclusion than acceptance.

In historical texts, we find vague descriptions of individuals who may have had autism, though the condition was not recognized as such. Terms like "idiocy" or "madness" were commonly used to describe people who could not conform to social norms or communicate in typical ways. Institutions became the primary "treatment" for such individuals, and these facilities were often places of neglect, isolation, and even abuse.

It's important to recognize that the lack of understanding wasn't due to malice but ignorance. The scientific and medical communities simply lacked the tools to identify and categorize autism. What we now see as a spectrum of neurological differences was viewed through the lens of mental illness or behavioral disorders.

Leo Kanner and the First Recognized Definition of Autism

The first major breakthrough in the understanding of autism came in 1943 when Dr. Leo Kanner, a child psychiatrist at Johns Hopkins University, published a landmark paper that described a group of children with distinct characteristics. Kanner's paper, titled "Autistic Disturbances of Affective Contact," outlined the behaviors of eleven children who exhibited what he described as a profound "inability to relate themselves in the ordinary way to people and situations." These children, he noted, appeared to live in their own worlds, avoiding social interactions, exhibiting a strong need for routine, and often showing repetitive behaviors.

Kanner's work was groundbreaking because it identified autism as a unique condition, separate from intellectual disability or schizophrenia, which had previously been used to describe these children's behaviors. For the first time, autism was recognized as its own disorder—something that affected the way children developed, communicated, and engaged with the world around them.

While Kanner's work was pioneering, it also came with certain limitations. Most notably, he attributed the cause of autism to cold, unloving parenting, particularly from mothers. This led to the "refrigerator mother" theory, which blamed mothers for their children's autism. This misguided belief caused profound emotional pain for many families, particularly mothers, who were wrongly held responsible for their children's condition. This erroneous theory persisted for decades before being debunked by subsequent research.

Despite these early missteps, Kanner's research laid the foundation for future studies of autism, helping to distinguish it as a separate developmental disorder. His observations about social withdrawal, repetitive behaviors, and resistance to change remain key components of the diagnostic criteria for Autism Spectrum Disorder (ASD) today.

Hans Asperger and High-Functioning Autism

Around the same time that Leo Kanner was conducting his research, Austrian pediatrician Hans Asperger was studying a group of children who exhibited similar but slightly different traits. In 1944, Asperger published a paper describing children who had difficulties with social interactions and communication but who also demonstrated strong language skills and specialized interests. Unlike Kanner's patients, who were often non-verbal and more severely affected, the children Asperger studied were verbal and often highly intelligent.

Asperger's work was largely unknown outside of Europe for several decades, and it wasn't until the 1980s that his research gained significant attention in the United States. Asperger's Syndrome, as it became known, was eventually recognized as a distinct condition within the broader autism spectrum. The children Asperger described were often seen as "high-functioning" because they could communicate verbally and had average or above-average intelligence, but they still struggled with the social and behavioral challenges characteristic of autism.

This distinction between Kanner's autism and Asperger's Syndrome helped broaden the understanding of autism as a spectrum. It became clear that individuals with autism could have a wide range of abilities and challenges, from non-verbal individuals with significant support needs to highly verbal individuals who struggled mainly with social interactions.

In 2013, the *Diagnostic and Statistical Manual of Mental Disorders* (DSM-5) merged Asperger's Syndrome into the broader category of

Autism Spectrum Disorder (ASD), reflecting the growing consensus that autism exists on a continuum rather than as a set of distinct categories. This shift was significant in recognizing the diversity of the autism experience, while also providing a more unified approach to diagnosis and treatment.

From Misunderstanding to Medical Progress

The decades following Kanner and Asperger's initial research were marked by both progress and setbacks. Throughout the 1950s and 1960s, autism was still largely misunderstood, and many children with autism were misdiagnosed with intellectual disabilities or mental illnesses. Treatments for autism were often rudimentary and based on a behavioral model that sought to correct or suppress "undesirable" behaviors rather than understanding the underlying neurological differences.

One of the more controversial treatments during this time was Applied Behavior Analysis (ABA), developed by psychologist Ivar Lovaas in the 1960s. ABA focused on using positive reinforcement to encourage desired behaviors and discourage unwanted ones. While ABA remains a widely used and effective therapy for some individuals with autism, it has also been criticized for its early use of aversive techniques (such as electric shocks) and for its focus on normalizing autistic behavior rather than supporting the individual's natural strengths and differences.

In the 1970s and 1980s, autism advocacy began to gain traction as parents and caregivers started to push back against the prevailing notions of institutionalization and punitive therapies. Organizations like the Autism Society of America were founded, giving families a voice and advocating for better treatment options, more research, and a shift away from the outdated "refrigerator mother" theory.

Advocacy groups also began raising awareness of the fact that autism was not a psychological condition that could be cured but a developmental disorder that required understanding, support, and early intervention.

During this time, research also began to focus on the biological and genetic underpinnings of autism. Scientists started to recognize that autism was not caused by cold parenting or psychological trauma but was instead rooted in differences in brain development. This shift in understanding was crucial in reshaping the way society viewed autism, allowing for more compassionate and science-based approaches to treatment and care.

The Neurodiversity Movement: A New Paradigm

The 1990s marked the beginning of a paradigm shift in how autism was viewed, thanks in large part to the neurodiversity movement. The term "neurodiversity" was coined by Australian sociologist Judy Singer in the late 1990s and refers to the idea that neurological differences, including autism, should be recognized and respected as natural variations of the human experience. The neurodiversity movement argues that autism is not a disorder to be cured or eradicated but a different way of thinking and being in the world.

This movement has had a profound impact on the autism community, particularly in terms of how autistic individuals advocate for themselves. Rather than focusing solely on the challenges or deficits associated with autism, neurodiversity emphasizes the strengths, talents, and unique perspectives that individuals with autism bring to the table. Many individuals on the spectrum have become outspoken advocates for their own rights, rejecting the notion that they are "broken" or in need of fixing.

The neurodiversity movement also highlights the importance of acceptance over mere awareness. While awareness campaigns have helped bring autism into the public consciousness, the neurodiversity movement calls for a deeper understanding of autism as a valuable part of human diversity. Advocates argue that society should adapt to accommodate the needs of autistic individuals, rather than forcing them to conform to neurotypical standards.

The Role of Advocacy and Awareness

In the late 20th and early 21st centuries, advocacy for individuals with autism reached new heights. The rise of organizations like Autism Speaks, the National Autistic Society, and the Autistic Self Advocacy Network (ASAN) has helped to amplify the voices of autistic individuals and their families, pushing for greater inclusion, better services, and more research funding.

Autism awareness campaigns have played a key role in educating the public about the challenges and strengths of individuals with autism. April is now recognized as Autism Awareness Month, and World Autism Awareness Day, celebrated on April 2nd, helps to bring global attention to the importance of early diagnosis, intervention, and acceptance. These campaigns have been instrumental in reducing the stigma associated with autism and promoting a more nuanced understanding of the condition.

However, while awareness has grown, there is still much work to be done. Many advocates now argue that society needs to move beyond awareness toward true acceptance and inclusion. Autistic individuals continue to face significant barriers in education, employment, healthcare, and social settings. Acceptance means not just recognizing the existence of autism but actively working to create a world where autistic individuals are respected, supported, and given the opportunity to thrive.

Scripture and the Strength of the Lord in Autism

As we reflect on the history of autism and the journey from misunderstanding to awareness, it's important to remember that, as Christians, we find strength in the Lord. In moments of struggle, doubt, or exhaustion, we can turn to scripture for encouragement and guidance, knowing that God's plan for each of us is perfect and purposeful—even when we don't fully understand it.

In Isaiah 43:1, the Lord says, *"Do not fear, for I have redeemed you; I have summoned you by name; you are mine."* This passage reminds us that every individual, including those with autism, is precious to God. He knows them by name and has called them for a purpose. The struggles of living with autism or raising a child with autism can be overwhelming at times, but we can rest in the knowledge that God is with us through it all. He has created each of us uniquely, and in His eyes, every person has inherent worth and dignity.

In 2 Corinthians 12:9, Paul writes, *"But he said to me, 'My grace is sufficient for you, for my power is made perfect in weakness.' Therefore I will boast all the more gladly of my weaknesses, so that the power of Christ may rest upon me."* For families and individuals facing the daily challenges of autism, this verse offers hope. It reminds us that God's strength is made perfect in our weaknesses, and in our most difficult moments, His grace is sufficient to carry us through.

The journey from misunderstanding to awareness is not just a societal or scientific one; it is also a deeply personal and spiritual journey for those living with autism and their loved ones. As we walk this path, we can find comfort in the words of Jeremiah 29:11: *"For I know the plans I have for you," declares the Lord, "plans to prosper you and not to harm you, plans to give you hope and a future."* No matter how difficult the journey may be, we can trust that God's plan is good, and He will bring hope and healing in His perfect time.

Conclusion: Moving Forward with Faith and Acceptance

The history of autism is one of progress, but it is also a reminder of the many challenges that individuals with autism and their families have faced along the way. From early misunderstandings and harmful treatments to the rise of advocacy and the neurodiversity movement, the journey from misunderstanding to awareness has been long and difficult.

As we move forward, it's essential to continue advocating for a world where individuals with autism are not just aware of their differences but are accepted and celebrated for who they are. And as Christians, we can draw strength from the Lord, knowing that He has a purpose for every life and that His love for each of us is boundless.

Autism is not a label to be feared or a condition to be fixed. It is a spectrum of human diversity, and in God's eyes, every person on that spectrum is wonderfully and fearfully made.

Here are some scripture references that align with the theme "The History of Autism: From Misunderstanding to Awareness"

1. Proverbs 18:15 (NIV)

"The heart of the discerning acquires knowledge, for the ears of the wise seek it out."

This verse emphasizes the pursuit of knowledge and understanding, encouraging a shift from ignorance or misunderstanding toward awareness and wisdom.

2. 1 Corinthians 13:12 (NIV)

"For now we see only a reflection as in a mirror; then we shall see face to face. Now I know in part; then I shall know fully, even as I am fully known."
This scripture highlights the progression from partial understanding to full awareness, much like the journey from misunderstanding to deeper knowledge of autism.

3. James 1:5 (NIV)

"If any of you lacks wisdom, you should ask God, who gives generously to all without finding fault, and it will be given to you."
This verse reminds us to seek wisdom and understanding from God, who can guide us in learning about autism and correcting past misconceptions.

4. Hosea 4:6 (NIV)

"My people are destroyed from lack of knowledge."
This passage reflects the consequences of ignorance, underscoring the importance of gaining knowledge and awareness about autism to overcome past misunderstandings.

5. Proverbs 4:7 (NIV)

"The beginning of wisdom is this: Get wisdom. Though it cost all you have, get understanding."
This verse encourages the pursuit of understanding, symbolizing the importance of education and awareness in moving from misunderstanding to enlightenment about autism.

These scriptures offer insights into the importance of seeking understanding, moving away from ignorance, and growing in compassion and awareness as we learn more about autism. They reflect the journey from misunderstanding to greater acceptance and empathy.

Chapter 23

Dispelling Myths Common Misconceptions About Autism

"Do not conform to the pattern of this world, but be transformed by the renewing of your mind."

Romans 12:2

Autism is one of the most misunderstood conditions in today's society, despite increasing awareness. Misconceptions and myths about autism can create barriers for individuals on the spectrum and their families, often leading to isolation, judgment, and frustration. These myths not only misrepresent the realities of living with autism but also overshadow the unique strengths and potential of autistic individuals. For families living with a loved one diagnosed with autism, navigating these misconceptions can add an extra layer of difficulty to an already challenging journey.

In this chapter, we will dispel some of the most common myths about autism, exploring the truths behind these misconceptions. Through the lens of faith and scripture, we will also draw on the strength and comfort that comes from our Lord and Savior, Jesus Christ, who reminds us that every person is beautifully and wonderfully made. In doing so, we aim to shift the conversation about autism from one of deficit and misunderstanding to one of acceptance, respect, and God's unconditional love.

Myth 1: "People with Autism Lack Empathy"

One of the most pervasive myths about autism is that individuals on the spectrum lack empathy or the ability to feel or express compassion for others. This misconception likely arises because many autistic individuals may struggle with reading social cues or responding to emotions in ways that neurotypical people expect. For example, someone with autism might not show facial expressions that align with what others assume empathy looks like, or they might have difficulty understanding non-verbal cues like body language.

However, the truth is that many individuals with autism experience deep empathy, sometimes even more acutely than neurotypical individuals. Some autistic people are highly sensitive to the emotions of others but may not know how to express their empathy outwardly. Emotional empathy—the ability to feel what another person is feeling—is present in many individuals with autism, even if cognitive empathy (understanding why someone feels a certain way) is more challenging.

As believers, we can look to scripture to remind us that empathy is not always about how emotions are expressed but about the heart behind the feelings. In Romans 12:15, we are instructed to *"Rejoice with those who rejoice; mourn with those who mourn."* This verse reflects the essence of empathy—being with others in their emotions, whether we express it outwardly or experience it quietly within ourselves. God sees the heart, and He understands that empathy can manifest in many ways.

Myth 2: "Autism Is Caused by Vaccines"

Perhaps one of the most harmful myths about autism is the belief that vaccines, particularly the MMR (measles, mumps, and rubella) vaccine, cause autism. This myth stems from a now-discredited study published in 1998 by Dr. Andrew Wakefield, which falsely claimed a link between vaccines and autism. Since then, extensive research has debunked this claim, and numerous studies have shown that there is no connection between vaccines and autism. However, this misinformation continues to circulate, leading to vaccine hesitancy and putting public health at risk.

The persistence of this myth has caused immense harm, not only by perpetuating fear about vaccines but also by diverting attention away from the real needs of individuals with autism and their families. Instead of focusing on support, education, and acceptance, this myth encourages a search for blame that can fracture relationships and communities.

As Christians, we are called to seek truth and avoid the spread of harmful falsehoods. Proverbs 12:22 reminds us that *"The Lord detests lying lips, but He delights in people who are trustworthy."* It is our responsibility to be discerning in the information we share and to stand against misinformation that causes harm. Trusting in the wisdom of God and the truths that science can reveal, we can reject the vaccine-autism myth and instead focus on what truly matters—supporting and loving those with autism.

Myth 3: "Autistic People Don't Want Friends or Relationships"

A common myth is that individuals with autism prefer to be alone and are uninterested in forming relationships. This misconception is based on the observation that many autistic people have difficulty with social interactions, such as understanding social cues, making eye contact, or engaging in small talk. However, this does not mean that people with autism do not desire meaningful friendships or connections. In fact, many individuals with autism deeply value relationships but may approach them in different ways.

Social interaction can be overwhelming for individuals on the spectrum due to sensory overload, anxiety, or difficulties with communication. As a result, some may prefer more structured social environments or one-on-one interactions rather than large group settings. Additionally, some autistic people may bond over shared interests or activities rather than traditional social exchanges like casual conversation.

Scripture teaches us about the importance of relationships and reminds us that we are all part of the body of Christ, each with unique gifts and ways of connecting with others. In 1 Corinthians 12:12, it says, *"Just as a body, though one, has many parts, but all its many parts form one body, so it is with Christ."* This verse encourages us to recognize that while we may interact with others differently, we are all valuable members of God's family. Relationships may look different for individuals with autism, but they are just as meaningful and important.

Myth 4: "Autism Is a Tragedy"

Autism is often viewed through a lens of tragedy, with many assuming that a diagnosis of autism brings only sadness and loss. This myth contributes to the narrative that autism is something to be "cured" or "fixed," rather than understood and embraced. While it's true that autism can bring significant challenges—especially in a world that is not always accommodating—this perspective ignores the strengths, talents, and unique perspectives that individuals with autism bring to the world.

Autism is not a tragedy, but a different way of being. Many individuals with autism have exceptional abilities in areas like mathematics, art, music, or memory. They often think creatively and approach problems from unique angles. These strengths are a reminder that God's creation is diverse, and every individual has a purpose.

Jeremiah 29:11 offers comfort and hope to all of us, including individuals with autism: *"For I know the plans I have for you," declares the Lord, "plans to prosper you and not to harm you, plans to give you hope and a future."* Autism is not a barrier to God's plans. In fact, individuals with autism often contribute to the world in profound and unexpected ways. Rather than viewing autism as a tragedy, we can celebrate the gifts that each person brings and trust in God's perfect plan for their lives.

Myth 5: "Autism Only Affects Children"

There is a common misconception that autism is a childhood condition, one that individuals may "outgrow" as they reach adulthood. This myth persists partly because autism is typically diagnosed in early childhood, and much of the focus in media and research is on children with autism. However, autism is a lifelong condition, and individuals on the spectrum continue to face challenges and opportunities throughout their lives.

As individuals with autism age, their needs may change, but the core aspects of autism remain. Some may become more adept at navigating social interactions or managing sensory sensitivities, while others may continue to require significant support. Many autistic adults face challenges related to employment, independent living, and forming relationships, particularly because services for adults with autism are often limited.

Scripture teaches us that we are called to support one another throughout all stages of life, not just during childhood. In Galatians

6:2, we are reminded to *"Carry each other's burdens, and in this way you will fulfill the law of Christ."* This verse speaks to the importance of lifelong support and care. As a community, we are called to walk alongside individuals with autism throughout their lives, offering compassion, understanding, and practical support as they navigate adulthood.

Myth 6: "People with Autism Can't Succeed in Life"

Another damaging myth is that individuals with autism cannot lead successful, independent lives. This misconception stems from a misunderstanding of autism as a limiting or disabling condition, rather than a spectrum that includes a wide range of abilities and challenges. While some individuals with autism may require significant support, many are capable of achieving great success in their careers, personal lives, and communities.

Autistic individuals have made significant contributions in fields like technology, art, science, and education. The success of individuals like Temple Grandin, a professor and animal behavior expert, or Satoshi Tajiri, the creator of Pokémon, are examples of how autistic individuals can thrive when their strengths are recognized and supported.

God has given each of us unique gifts and talents, and autism does not diminish those gifts. In 1 Peter 4:10, we are told, *"Each of you should use whatever gift you have received to serve others, as faithful stewards of God's grace in its various forms."* This scripture reminds us that we all have a purpose, and individuals with autism are no exception. By embracing their strengths and offering the support they need, we can help them fulfill their God-given potential.

Myth 7: "Autism Is Caused by Bad Parenting"

The idea that autism is caused by bad parenting, particularly cold or neglectful mothers, is a harmful myth that gained traction in the 1940s and 1950s. Psychologists like Dr. Leo Kanner popularized the "refrigerator mother" theory, which claimed that emotionally distant parents were responsible for their children's autism. This theory has since been thoroughly debunked, but its effects linger, causing unnecessary guilt and shame for parents.

Research has shown that autism is a neurodevelopmental condition with a strong genetic component. Parenting style does not cause autism, and individuals with autism are born with the condition. While early intervention and supportive parenting can make a positive difference in helping children with autism develop skills, the root cause of autism lies in the brain's wiring, not in how a child is raised.

As Christians, we are called to lift up and support families, not burden them with blame or judgment. In Psalm 127:3, we read, *"Children are a heritage from the Lord, offspring a reward from him."* This verse reminds us that all children, including those with autism, are gifts from God. Parents of children with autism should be encouraged, loved, and supported, not blamed for something beyond their control.

Myth 8: "All People with Autism Are the Same"

One of the most damaging misconceptions about autism is the belief that all individuals on the spectrum are the same. Autism is often portrayed in the media through limited stereotypes—either as people with severe disabilities or as "autistic savants" with extraordinary abilities. These narrow portrayals ignore the vast diversity within the autism spectrum and reduce individuals to a label rather than recognizing them as unique people with varied strengths, challenges, and personalities.

Autism is a spectrum, meaning that individuals with autism experience it in many different ways. Some may be non-verbal, while others may have highly developed language skills. Some may excel in areas like mathematics or music, while others may struggle with daily tasks. No two people with autism are alike, and their experiences, challenges, and gifts are as diverse as those of the neurotypical population.

In 1 Corinthians 12:4-6, we are reminded that *"There are different kinds of gifts, but the same Spirit distributes them. There are different kinds of service, but the same Lord. There are different kinds of working, but in all of them and in everyone it is the same God at work."* This scripture encourages us to recognize the diversity of gifts and abilities in every person, including those with autism. Each individual is created in the image of God, with their own unique purpose and potential.

Moving Toward Acceptance

Dispelling these myths about autism is essential for building a more inclusive and compassionate society. By rejecting false beliefs and embracing the truth, we can create an environment where individuals with autism are understood, supported, and valued for who they are. Autism is not a label to be feared, but a different way of experiencing the world, one that is rich in diversity and potential.

As we walk alongside our loved ones with autism, let us draw strength from our faith in the Lord. In Isaiah 41:10, God promises, *"So do not fear, for I am with you; do not be dismayed, for I am your God. I will strengthen you and help you; I will uphold you with my righteous right hand."* This assurance reminds us that we are never alone in our journey, and that God's love and strength will guide us every step of the way.

By dispelling the myths surrounding autism and embracing the truths of our faith, we can build a world where all individuals, regardless of ability, are seen, loved, and cherished as the beautiful creations of God they are.

Here are some scripture references that align with the theme "Dispelling Myths: Common Misconceptions About Autism" for Chapter 1:

1. John 7:24 (NIV)

"Stop judging by mere appearances, but instead judge correctly."
This verse encourages people to look beyond surface-level judgments and seek truth, helping dispel myths and misconceptions by seeing deeper than outward appearances.

2. James 1:5 (NIV)

"If any of you lacks wisdom, you should ask God, who gives generously to all without finding fault, and it will be given to you."
God offers wisdom to those who seek it, which can guide us in understanding autism correctly, clearing up confusion or misconceptions.

3. Proverbs 18:15 (NIV)

"The heart of the discerning acquires knowledge, for the ears of the wise seek it out."
This verse underscores the importance of seeking knowledge and truth, urging us to learn and discern rather than rely on myths or misinformation.

4. Isaiah 11:3 (NIV)

"He will not judge by what he sees with his eyes, or decide by what he hears with his ears."
This verse reflects the importance of not basing judgments on outward appearances or hearsay, reminding us to seek deeper understanding beyond misconceptions.

5. Hosea 4:6 (NIV)

"My people are destroyed from lack of knowledge."
This verse emphasizes the dangers of ignorance and the importance of seeking knowledge, especially in correcting false assumptions and myths about autism.

These scriptures emphasize the importance of seeking truth, wisdom, and understanding to dispel myths and misconceptions about autism. They encourage clarity, honesty, and a deeper knowledge that replaces ignorance with compassion and truth.

Chapter 24

Communication and Social Interaction—Beyond Verbal Cues

"So is my word that goes out from my mouth: It will not return to me empty, but will accomplish what I desire and achieve the purpose for which I sent it."

Isaiah 55:11

Communication is one of the most profound and essential aspects of human interaction. It allows us to connect, express feelings, share ideas, and build relationships. However, for individuals on the autism spectrum, communication often looks different. Many people with autism experience challenges with traditional verbal communication, relying instead on alternative forms of expression, such as non-verbal cues, body language, written communication, or even artistic outlets like drawing, music, or movement.

For families living with a loved one diagnosed with autism, these differences in communication can be both a challenge and a revelation. The key lies in understanding that communication goes beyond words. It's about connection, mutual understanding, and finding ways to bridge the gaps that language can sometimes create. This chapter will explore how individuals with autism navigate communication and social interaction in ways that transcend verbal cues. We will also look to scripture for guidance, finding strength in the Lord as we embrace these differences and deepen our understanding of true connection.

The Spectrum of Communication in Autism

Autism exists on a spectrum, and communication abilities can vary widely from person to person. Some individuals with autism are non-verbal, meaning they may not use spoken language to communicate at all. Others may have highly developed verbal skills but struggle with understanding social nuances, interpreting body language, or engaging in back-and-forth conversation. Some individuals on the spectrum may rely on assistive communication devices or sign language, while others might use written communication or pictures to express themselves.

One of the most significant misconceptions about individuals with autism is the belief that those who are non-verbal do not want to communicate or are incapable of expressing their thoughts and emotions. This could not be further from the truth. Non-verbal individuals often have a rich inner world and can communicate effectively through alternative means, including gestures, facial expressions, and other non-verbal cues.

The story of Moses reminds us that even when verbal communication is challenging, God provides ways for us to fulfill His purpose. When Moses was called by God to lead the Israelites out of Egypt, he expressed concern about his ability to speak. In Exodus 4:10-12, Moses said, *"Pardon your servant, Lord. I have never been eloquent, neither in the past nor since you have spoken to your servant. I am slow of speech and tongue."* But the Lord responded, *"Who gave human beings their mouths? Who makes them deaf or mute? Who gives them sight or makes them blind? Is it not I, the Lord? Now go; I will help you speak and will teach you what to say."*

This passage reminds us that God equips each of us with unique ways to communicate, and no one is limited by their ability to speak. Just as Moses found a way to fulfill God's mission, individuals with autism find ways to connect with others, even when verbal communication is difficult.

Non-Verbal Communication: Understanding Without Words

For many individuals with autism, non-verbal communication is a primary mode of interaction. Non-verbal cues such as eye contact, facial expressions, gestures, and body language can convey as much—if not more—than words. However, the interpretation of these non-verbal cues may differ for individuals on the spectrum, both in how they express themselves and in how they understand the cues of others.

Eye contact, for example, is often considered a crucial part of communication in many cultures. However, for some individuals with autism, maintaining eye contact can be uncomfortable, overwhelming, or distracting. Avoiding eye contact does not mean that the person is disinterested or disengaged; rather, it may be a way for them to better focus on the conversation or process what is being said without sensory overload.

Similarly, autistic individuals may express emotions through more subtle or unconventional gestures. For example, instead of smiling or laughing when they are happy, they may engage in behaviors such as hand-flapping, rocking, or other repetitive movements. These actions, often referred to as "stimming," are not merely habits but ways of regulating sensory input and expressing feelings.

The Bible teaches us to look beyond appearances and focus on the heart. In 1 Samuel 16:7, the Lord says to Samuel, *"Do not consider his appearance or his height, for I have rejected him. The Lord does not look at the things people look at. People look at the outward appearance, but the Lord looks at the heart."* This scripture encourages us to see beyond the surface, to look deeper than the outward behaviors of individuals with autism, and to understand the heart and intent behind their actions.

Non-verbal communication is a powerful form of expression, and families can learn to recognize and respond to these cues with patience and understanding. By paying attention to the unique ways their loved ones communicate, they can build stronger connections and foster deeper relationships.

The Challenges of Social Interaction

Social interaction presents its own set of challenges for individuals with autism. While neurotypical individuals often navigate social situations instinctively, those on the autism spectrum may need to work harder to understand the unspoken rules and expectations of social engagement. This can include interpreting tone of voice, understanding sarcasm or metaphor, and recognizing social cues like personal space, body language, or conversational timing.

Many individuals with autism struggle with what is known as "social reciprocity," or the give-and-take of social interactions. Conversations can feel like a puzzle, with many unspoken rules that are hard to follow. For example, knowing when to speak, how long to hold a conversation, or how to interpret humor or idiomatic expressions can be overwhelming for someone on the spectrum.

However, just because social interactions can be challenging does not mean that individuals with autism do not want to engage. In fact, many people on the spectrum desire connection and friendships but may express their interest in different ways. They may find comfort in structured social situations, where the expectations are clear, or they may connect with others over shared interests and activities rather than small talk.

The Bible provides guidance on how we are to approach relationships, offering wisdom that can be applied to our understanding of social interaction. In Philippians 2:3-4, we are told, *"Do nothing out of selfish ambition or vain conceit. Rather, in humility value others above yourselves, not looking to your own interests but each of you to the interests of the others."* This verse reminds us to approach social interactions with patience, understanding, and a willingness to meet people where they are, especially when those interactions may not follow the conventional patterns we expect.

Assistive Technology and Alternative Communication

For individuals who are non-verbal or have limited verbal communication, assistive technology has opened up new possibilities for expression and connection. Communication devices, such as speech-generating devices (SGDs), tablets with specialized apps, and picture exchange communication systems (PECS), provide alternative ways for individuals with autism to express their thoughts, needs, and emotions.

These technologies empower individuals to engage with the world around them in ways that might have been inaccessible before. For many, the ability to communicate through technology offers a sense of autonomy and freedom, allowing them to express themselves clearly without relying on verbal speech.

The impact of assistive technology cannot be overstated. For families, watching their loved ones use these tools to communicate can be a powerful and emotional experience. The ability to hear someone's thoughts—whether through a device or a typed message—can strengthen relationships and provide insight into the individual's inner world.

In Psalm 139:1-4, David writes, *"You have searched me, Lord, and you know me. You know when I sit and when I rise; you perceive my thoughts from afar. You discern my going out and my lying down; you are familiar with all my ways. Before a word is on my tongue you, Lord, know it completely."* This passage serves as a reminder that God knows us deeply, even before we speak. In the same way, families can learn to understand their loved ones' needs, even when those needs are communicated in non-traditional ways.

Assistive technology can be a powerful tool, but it's important to recognize that communication is about more than words. Families should continue to foster connection through gestures, eye contact, shared activities, and simply being present with their loved ones. These moments of connection, though sometimes quiet, are meaningful and can build lasting bonds.

The Power of Written and Artistic Communication

For some individuals with autism, writing or artistic expression provides a preferred method of communication. Writing allows individuals to organize their thoughts, express complex emotions, and share their inner world with others in a way that may feel more comfortable or natural than spoken language.

Many individuals on the autism spectrum have exceptional artistic abilities and use visual arts, music, or other creative outlets to communicate. Art can serve as a language of its own, allowing individuals to express themselves without the constraints of verbal speech. For some, drawing, painting, or creating music is not only a form of self-expression but also a way to process emotions, manage sensory experiences, and connect with others on a deeper level.

Artistic and written communication are gifts from God, allowing people to transcend the limitations of spoken language. In Ephesians 2:10, we are reminded, *"For we are God's handiwork, created in Christ Jesus to do good works, which God prepared in advance for us to do."* This verse speaks to the creative potential within each of us. Individuals with autism often have unique ways of expressing their creativity, and these gifts should be celebrated and nurtured.

Families can encourage their loved ones to explore different forms of expression, whether through writing, drawing, music, or other creative outlets. These alternative forms of communication can reveal a wealth of insight and beauty, helping families better understand and appreciate the richness of their loved ones' inner world.

Social Connections Through Shared Interests

One of the most effective ways for individuals with autism to build social connections is through shared interests. Many people on the spectrum have focused or specialized interests in specific topics, such as trains, animals, technology, or art. These interests can serve as bridges for social interaction, allowing individuals to connect with others who share similar passions.

For families, finding ways to support and engage with these interests can lead to meaningful connections and deeper relationships. Whether it's attending a train exhibition, exploring a favorite book series, or building a model together, these shared experiences create opportunities for bonding and communication.

The Bible teaches us the value of companionship and shared experience. In Ecclesiastes 4:9-10, we read, *"Two are better than one, because they have a good return for their labor: If either of them falls down, one can help the other up. But pity anyone who falls and has no one to help them up."* This verse reminds us that connection and companionship are essential for our well-being. By engaging in activities that bring joy and comfort to our loved ones, we can foster connection and support their social development.

Strength in the Lord: Embracing Differences in Communication

For families living with a loved one diagnosed with autism, embracing differences in communication can be a transformative experience. It requires patience, understanding, and a willingness to look beyond verbal cues to recognize the many ways that connection can occur. While this journey may come with challenges, it is also filled with moments of grace and beauty.

As Christians, we find strength and guidance in our Lord and Savior. In Proverbs 3:5-6, we are reminded to *"Trust in the Lord with all your heart and lean not on your own understanding; in all your ways submit to him, and he will make your paths straight."* This verse encourages us to trust in God's plan, even when we do not fully understand it. Communication may look different for individuals with autism, but God's love transcends all forms of expression. He understands our hearts, our thoughts, and our desires, even when they are not spoken.

In this journey, we are reminded that communication is about connection, not perfection. Just as God meets us where we are, we can meet our loved ones with autism where they are, embracing their unique ways of interacting with the world. Through love, patience, and faith, we can foster deep and meaningful relationships that go beyond verbal cues.

By dispelling the myths and misunderstandings surrounding autism and communication, we can build a more compassionate and inclusive world where every person's voice is heard—whether through words, gestures, art, or the quiet language of presence. And in all things, we trust in the strength and guidance of our Lord, who walks with us every step of the way.

Here are some scripture references that align with the theme "Communication and Social Interaction—Beyond Verbal Cues"

1. Psalm 19:1-2 (NIV)

"The heavens declare the glory of God; the skies proclaim the work of his hands. Day after day they pour forth speech; night after night they reveal knowledge."
This passage emphasizes that communication doesn't always need words—creation itself speaks of God's glory, just as meaningful communication can happen beyond verbal cues.

2. Romans 8:26 (NIV)

"In the same way, the Spirit helps us in our weakness. We do not know what we ought to pray for, but the Spirit himself intercedes for us through wordless groans."
Even without words, God understands our hearts. This verse illustrates that true communication goes beyond spoken language, highlighting the power of non-verbal interaction.

3. 1 Samuel 16:7 (NIV)

"But the Lord said to Samuel, 'Do not consider his appearance or his height, for I have rejected him. The Lord does not look at the things people look at. People look at the outward appearance, but the Lord looks at the heart.'"
This scripture reminds us that communication and connection go deeper than what is outwardly expressed. God sees and understands the heart, just as we can communicate through actions and emotions beyond words.

4. Proverbs 3:5-6 (NIV)

"Trust in the Lord with all your heart and lean not on your own understanding; in all your ways submit to him, and he will make your paths straight."
This passage emphasizes trusting in God's deeper understanding beyond what is immediately seen or heard, much like how effective communication often happens beyond verbal interaction.

5. James 1:19 (NIV)

"My dear brothers and sisters, take note of this: Everyone should be quick to listen, slow to speak and slow to become angry."
Listening and observing are crucial for understanding others beyond verbal cues, underscoring the importance of attentiveness in communication.

These scriptures emphasize that communication extends beyond verbal expression, reflecting that meaningful interaction can happen through actions, emotions, and even stillness. They align with the theme of understanding different ways of connecting with others, especially when language might not be the primary form of communication.

Chapter 25

Family Dynamics: Growing Together

"Be completely humble and gentle; be patient, bearing with one another in love. Make every effort to keep the unity of the Spirit through the bond of peace."

Ephesians 4:2-3

Introduction:

The Family as a Foundation of Support

Family is the first community that we belong to. It is a place of love, guidance, and shared experiences, but when a family has a member on the autism spectrum, the dynamics often require adaptation and growth. Autism brings challenges that can test the resilience and unity of a family, but it also reveals strengths that might otherwise remain hidden. By embracing both the struggles and the gifts that autism brings, families can grow together, learning new ways to support one another, celebrate diversity, and build a stronger, more inclusive foundation.

In this chapter, *Family Dynamics: Growing Together*, we will explore how autism impacts family relationships, emphasizing the importance of open communication, patience, and faith. We'll discuss the ways in which autism can reshape family life, the challenges and rewards that come with it, and the role that scripture can play in providing strength and guidance. With a foundation of love and faith, families can not only survive the difficulties but also thrive, growing closer and stronger as they navigate the unique journey of raising a child with autism.

The Bible provides us with wisdom on how to approach challenges with love, patience, and humility. Ephesians 4:2 reminds us to "be completely humble and gentle; be patient, bearing with one another in love." This verse encapsulates the heart of family life, especially when raising a child on the spectrum. Love, patience, and humility are the cornerstones of a family that grows together through adversity, supported by their faith in God's plan.

1. Autism's Impact on Family Dynamics

a. The Emotional Journey for Parents: From Uncertainty to Understanding

For parents, receiving an autism diagnosis for their child often feels like the beginning of a long, emotional journey. The initial reaction may include shock, grief, or fear of the unknown. These feelings are normal and valid, as many parents find themselves grappling with how autism will affect their child's future, family life, and their own role as caregivers.

Proverbs 3:5-6 offers guidance during times of uncertainty: "Trust in the Lord with all your heart and lean not on your own understanding; in all your ways submit to him, and he will make your paths straight." This scripture reminds parents to lean on God's wisdom when they feel unsure of how to navigate their child's needs. Trusting in God's plan allows them to find peace amid the challenges, knowing that He will guide their family's journey.

Over time, many parents shift from feelings of uncertainty to a deeper understanding and appreciation of their child's unique qualities. They learn to advocate for their child's needs, celebrate their strengths, and embrace the differences that autism brings to their family life. This shift is a testament to the resilience and adaptability that parents develop as they grow alongside their child.

b. The Sibling Experience: A Blend of Love and Challenge

Siblings of children with autism often find themselves navigating complex emotions. On one hand, they may feel a strong bond with their autistic sibling, developing a deep sense of empathy and love. On the other hand, they may experience feelings of frustration, confusion, or even resentment, particularly when their sibling's needs take priority in the family dynamic.

Ephesians 4:32 encourages us to "be kind and compassionate to one another, forgiving each other, just as in Christ God forgave you." This scripture is especially relevant for siblings, who must learn to navigate moments of misunderstanding or frustration with compassion and forgiveness. By fostering an environment of kindness and support, siblings can grow together, learning valuable life lessons about patience, empathy, and unconditional love.

Siblings often become advocates and protectors, learning to stand up for their autistic brother or sister in social situations. This advocacy role can be empowering, giving siblings a sense of purpose and responsibility. However, it is essential for parents to recognize the unique challenges siblings face and to ensure that their emotional needs are also being met. By creating space for open communication and providing individual attention, parents can help siblings feel valued and supported.

2. Strengthening the Family Through Faith

a. Leaning on Scripture for Guidance and Strength

Faith is a powerful source of strength for families navigating the complexities of autism. The Bible offers numerous verses that provide comfort, guidance, and hope, reminding families that they are not alone in their journey. One of the most comforting scriptures is found in Isaiah 41:10, which says, "So do not fear, for I am with you; do not be dismayed, for I am your God. I will strengthen you and help you; I will uphold you with my righteous right hand." This verse reassures families that God is always present, providing strength and support in times of need.

Prayer also plays a crucial role in strengthening family bonds. Families who pray together often find solace in their shared faith, knowing that God hears their concerns and provides guidance. Whether they are praying for patience during difficult moments, wisdom in making decisions, or peace in their hearts, families can find comfort in knowing that their prayers are heard.

Additionally, families can find inspiration in the story of Job, who faced immense challenges but remained faithful to God. Job's perseverance is a reminder that, even in the face of adversity, faith can carry us through. Just as Job's faith was tested, so too are families tested by the challenges of autism, but with faith, they can emerge stronger and more united.

b. Trusting in God's Plan for Each Family Member

Autism often leads families to question why they have been given this particular challenge. While it's natural to wonder about God's plan, it is important to remember that every family member, including the individual with autism, has a unique purpose. Jeremiah 29:11 provides reassurance: "'For I know the plans I have for you,' declares the Lord, 'plans to prosper you and not to harm you, plans to give you hope and a future.'" This scripture reminds us that God's plan is one of hope and prosperity, even when the path seems difficult.

For the individual with autism, God's plan may involve using their unique gifts to inspire others, teach valuable lessons about compassion, or break down societal barriers. While the journey may be challenging, it is filled with opportunities for growth and purpose.

Families must trust that God's plan includes each member of the family, and that their experiences with autism are shaping them in ways that align with His greater purpose. Whether it's learning patience, developing advocacy skills, or fostering empathy, each family member plays a role in fulfilling God's plan for their family.

3. Building Stronger Communication Within the Family

a. Understanding Nonverbal Communication: A New Way to Connect

For many individuals on the autism spectrum, communication may look different from the traditional verbal exchange. Nonverbal communication, whether through gestures, body language, or alternative communication methods like AAC devices, is an essential aspect of connecting with a family member with autism. While this can be challenging for families accustomed to relying on verbal communication, it opens the door to new ways of understanding and connection.

James 1:19 advises us to "be quick to listen, slow to speak and slow to become angry." This scripture encourages families to be patient and attentive when communicating with their autistic family member. Rather than focusing on the absence of verbal language, families can learn to listen in new ways, paying attention to the unique forms of expression that their autistic family member uses. Whether it's through eye contact, gestures, or the use of visual aids, communication can take many forms, and it's up to the family to adapt and grow in their understanding.

By embracing nonverbal communication methods, families can create a more inclusive and supportive environment for their autistic member, fostering deeper connections that transcend traditional language barriers.

b. Overcoming Emotional Challenges: Managing Stress and Anxiety

Emotional regulation can be a significant challenge for individuals with autism, leading to moments of stress, anxiety, or meltdowns. For families, these moments can be difficult to navigate, as they try to soothe their loved one while managing their own emotional responses. In these moments, it's important for families to rely on their faith and trust in God's ability to provide peace.

Philippians 4:6-7 offers wisdom for managing anxiety: "Do not be anxious about anything, but in every situation, by prayer and petition, with thanksgiving, present your requests to God. And the peace of God, which transcends all understanding, will guard your hearts and your minds in Christ Jesus." This scripture reminds families to turn to prayer in times of stress, seeking God's peace to help them navigate difficult emotions.

Creating a calm, structured environment at home can also help individuals with autism manage their emotions more effectively. This might involve developing routines, using sensory tools, or establishing quiet spaces where the individual can retreat when feeling overwhelmed. By working together to understand and meet their autistic family member's emotional needs, families can create a more harmonious and supportive home environment.

4. Celebrating Strengths and Unique Gifts

a. Recognizing the Gifts of Autism

While autism presents challenges, it also brings unique strengths that should be celebrated within the family. Many individuals on the spectrum possess extraordinary talents, whether it's a keen attention to detail, a deep passion for a particular subject, or an incredible memory. These gifts are part of what makes individuals with autism so remarkable, and families can find joy in recognizing and nurturing these strengths.

1 Peter 4:10 reminds us that "each of you should use whatever gift you have received to serve others, as faithful stewards of God's grace in its various forms." This scripture encourages families to view their autistic family member's talents as gifts from God, meant to be shared and celebrated. Whether it's a talent for art, music, or problem-solving, these strengths can enrich the family dynamic and provide opportunities for growth and connection.

By focusing on the strengths and unique gifts that autism brings, families can shift their perspective from one of challenge to one of celebration. This positive outlook not only benefits the autistic individual but also strengthens the family as a whole, fostering a spirit of gratitude and joy.

b. Creating an Inclusive Environment for Growth

To help their autistic family member thrive, families must create an environment that is inclusive and supportive of their unique needs. This might involve making adjustments to the home environment, such as using visual schedules, minimizing sensory triggers, or incorporating alternative communication methods. It also involves advocating for inclusivity in the broader community, whether at school, church, or social events.

Romans 15:7 encourages us to "accept one another, then, just as Christ accepted you, in order to bring praise to God." This scripture highlights the importance of acceptance and inclusion, both within the family and beyond. By creating an inclusive environment, families not only support their autistic family member but also model Christ's love and acceptance for others.

When families commit to creating an environment where every member is valued and supported, they foster a sense of belonging that empowers their autistic family member to grow and thrive.

Conclusion: Growing Together Through Love and Faith

Autism presents unique challenges for families, but it also offers profound opportunities for growth, understanding, and love. By embracing the differences that autism brings, families can grow together, learning new ways to support one another and deepen their faith. Scripture provides wisdom and guidance for navigating these challenges, reminding families to trust in God's plan and lean on Him for strength.

As families grow together through the ups and downs of raising a child with autism, they discover new depths of love, patience, and resilience. With faith as their foundation, they can not only overcome the challenges but also celebrate the strengths and gifts that autism brings to their lives. In the end, it is love, rooted in faith, that helps families grow together—stronger, more compassionate, and united in their shared journey.

Here are some scripture references that align with the theme "Family Dynamics: Growing Together"

1. Colossians 3:13-14 (NIV)

2. Ephesians 4:2-3 (NIV)

"Be completely humble and gentle; be patient, bearing with one another in love. Make every effort to keep the unity of the Spirit through the bond of peace."
This verse encourages humility, gentleness, and patience, foundational traits for family members to grow together in harmony and peace.

3. Proverbs 22:6 (NIV)

"Start children off on the way they should go, and even when they are old they will not turn from it."
This verse highlights the role of family in nurturing and guiding children as they grow, laying a foundation for growth and unity as a family moves through different stages of life.

4. 1 Thessalonians 5:11 (NIV)

"Therefore encourage one another and build each other up, just as in fact you are doing."
Families that encourage and support each other grow stronger, fostering a dynamic of mutual care and growth within the family unit.

5. Psalm 133:1 (NIV)

"How good and pleasant it is when God's people live together in unity!"
This verse emphasizes the beauty of living in harmony, something families can strive for as they grow together in understanding, love, and faith.

These scriptures emphasize the importance of love, support, unity, and mutual growth within family dynamics, encouraging a healthy and nurturing environment where families can thrive together.

Final Words

The Importance of Giving Your Life to Christ

Life is full of challenges, heartbreak, and moments of joy. But without Christ, even the brightest moments can feel fleeting, and the hardest struggles can feel overwhelming. When we give our lives to Christ, we step into a relationship that offers hope, strength, and eternal life, no matter what we face. Giving our lives to Christ is about surrender, about handing over control to the One who loves us, knows us, and created us for a purpose.

This step of faith isn't just a single decision but a daily journey of choosing to follow Jesus, leaning on Him in all things. It begins with a moment of surrender, a prayer in which we acknowledge our sins and our need for a Savior. This is the *Sinner's Prayer*, a heartfelt declaration to let Jesus into our lives and allow Him to transform us from the inside out. Romans 10:9 reminds us of the simplicity and power of this act of faith: "**If you declare with your mouth, 'Jesus is Lord,' and believe in your heart that God raised him from the dead, you will be saved.**"

We'll explore why giving your life to Christ is the most important decision you'll ever make. And if you haven't taken this step yet, we'll walk through the Sinner's Prayer together, using God's Word as our foundation.

Why We Need Christ

From the beginning, God created us for a relationship with Him, but sin created a barrier between us and our Creator. Romans 3:23 tells us, "**For all have sinned and fall short of the glory of God.**" Sin isn't just about wrong actions or mistakes—it's a condition that separates us from God and brings death into our lives. This separation leaves an emptiness that we try to fill with temporary things, but only Jesus can fill the void.

Yet, even though we are sinners, God's love for us never fails. Romans 5:8 assures us of this: "**But God demonstrates his own love for us in this: While we were still sinners, Christ died for us.**" This love led Jesus to willingly go to the cross, taking the punishment we deserved and offering us new life through His resurrection. His sacrifice bridged the gap between us and God, making a way for us to be reconciled with Him.

Surrendering Control

Giving your life to Christ means surrendering control, acknowledging that you are no longer the leader of your own life. It's about trusting God with your past, present, and future, knowing that He has a plan for you. Proverbs 3:5-6 captures this perfectly: "**Trust in the Lord with all your heart and lean not on your own understanding; in all your ways submit to him, and he will make your paths straight.**"

Surrendering can be challenging. Many of us are used to being self-reliant, handling our problems on our own, and leaning on our own understanding. But Christ invites us to let go, to rest in His strength, and to allow Him to guide us. This isn't a sign of weakness; it's a declaration of trust in the One who holds all power and wisdom.

Accepting His Forgiveness and Grace

When we come to Christ, we bring with us our past mistakes, regrets, and failures. But in Christ, we find forgiveness, not condemnation. 1 John 1:9 tells us, "**If we confess our sins, he is faithful and just and will forgive us our sins and purify us**

from all unrighteousness." Jesus' forgiveness is complete; it cleanses us from every sin, no matter how big or small, and makes us new.

This forgiveness is a gift of grace—something we didn't earn and can never repay. Ephesians 2:8-9 reminds us, "For it is by grace you have been saved, through faith—and this is not from yourselves, it is the gift of God—not by works, so that no one can boast." God's grace covers all of our sins, inviting us into a relationship with Him that's based on love, not on what we can do. All we need to do is accept this gift.

A New Life in Christ

When we give our lives to Christ, we become new creations. 2 Corinthians 5:17 assures us of this transformation: "**Therefore, if anyone is in Christ, the new creation has come: The old has gone, the new is here!**" This doesn't mean that all of our problems will disappear or that life will suddenly be easy. But it does mean that we no longer face our struggles alone. Christ is with us, guiding us, strengthening us, and filling us with His peace.

As we walk with Christ, He transforms us from the inside out. He gives us a new purpose, a new identity, and the power to overcome sin. We begin to experience the abundant life He promised in John 10:10: "I have come that they may have life and have it to the full."

Walking Through the Sinner's Prayer

If you're ready to give your life to Christ, it begins with a simple prayer, often called the *Sinner's Prayer.* This prayer isn't about specific words; it's about the sincerity of your heart. The Sinner's Prayer is a way to express your faith, to confess your sins, and to invite Jesus to be Lord of your life.

Here's a step-by-step guide through the prayer, along with scriptures that support each part of the journey:

1. Acknowledge Your Need for a Savior

Begin by acknowledging that you are a sinner and that you need Jesus to save you. This is an act of humility, recognizing that you can't save yourself and that you need God's grace. Romans 3:23 says, "**For all have sinned and fall short of the glory of God.**"

Prayer:
"Lord, I know that I am a sinner. I know that I have made mistakes and that my sins have separated me from You. I recognize that I cannot fix this on my own and that I need Your forgiveness."

2. Believe in Jesus' Sacrifice and Resurrection

The next step is to believe that Jesus died for your sins and that He rose again, conquering sin and death. This is the foundation of our faith. Romans 10:9 assures us, "If you declare with your mouth, 'Jesus is Lord,' and believe in your heart that God raised him from the dead, you will be saved."

Prayer:
"I believe that Jesus died on the cross for my sins and that He rose again, defeating death and giving me the gift of eternal life. I believe that through His sacrifice, I am forgiven and made new."

3. Confess Jesus as Lord

Confessing Jesus as Lord means acknowledging Him as the ruler of your life. It's a declaration that you will follow Him and trust Him to lead you. 1 Corinthians 12:3 tells us, "No one can say, 'Jesus is Lord,' except by the Holy Spirit."

Prayer:
"Jesus, I confess that You are Lord. I surrender my life to You, trusting that You will guide me and transform me. I choose to follow You and live for You from this day forward."

4. Ask for Forgiveness and New Life

In this moment, ask God to forgive you for your sins and to make you new. This is where we receive the gift of God's grace, letting go of our past and stepping into a new life. Acts 3:19 says, "Repent, then, and turn to God, so that your sins may be wiped out, that times of refreshing may come from the Lord."

Prayer:
"Lord, please forgive me for my sins. Wash me clean, and fill me with Your Spirit. I turn away from my old life, and I ask You to help me walk in Your ways. Make me a new creation, filled with Your love, peace, and purpose."

5. Thank God for His Salvation

Finally, thank God for His salvation and the new life He has given you. Ephesians 2:8-9 reminds us that this is a gift from God: "**For it is by grace you have been saved, through faith—and this is not from yourselves, it is the gift of God—not by works, so that no one can boast.**"

Prayer:
"Thank You, God, for saving me. Thank You for Your love, Your forgiveness, and Your grace. I am so grateful that You have given me a new life, and I look forward to walking with You. In Jesus' name, Amen."

Embracing Your New Life in Christ

If you prayed that prayer, you have begun a journey that will change your life forever. This is the beginning of a relationship with Jesus, one that will grow and deepen over time. You are now a part of God's family, and He promises to be with you every step of the way.

Romans 8:38-39 assures us of God's unwavering love: "**For I am convinced that neither death nor life, neither angels nor demons, neither the present nor the future, nor any powers, neither height nor depth, nor anything else in all creation, will be able to separate us from the love of God that is in Christ Jesus our Lord.**" Nothing can separate you from His love. No matter what happens, He is with you, guiding you, and helping you grow in faith.

Walking Daily with Christ

Giving your life to Christ isn't just a single moment; it's the beginning of a lifelong journey. Each day, you will have the opportunity to draw closer to Him, to learn more about His love, and to trust Him with every part of your life. Spend time reading God's Word, praying, and surrounding yourself with other believers who can encourage and support you.

Remember that you are not alone. Jesus is with you, and He promises to never leave you nor forsake you (Hebrews 13:5). As you walk with Him, you will discover the joy, peace, and purpose that only He can give. In Him, you have a hope that transcends all circumstances, and a love that will carry you through every season of life.

Giving your life to Christ is the most important decision you can make. It is a step of faith, a leap into the arms of a Savior who loves you more than you can imagine. And as you walk with Him, you will find that He is more than enough for every challenge, every heartache, and every moment of your life.

www.ingramcontent.com/pod-product-compliance
Lightning Source LLC
LaVergne TN
LVHW100258210926
848480LV00003B/955
* 9 7 9 8 2 3 0 8 4 4 3 6 5 *